STRUCK DOWN, BUT NOT DESTROYED

MARIE ROSE

CrossBooks™
A Division of LifeWay
1663 Liberty Drive
Bloomington, IN 47403
www.crossbooks.com
Phone: 1-866-879-0502

© 2014 Marie Rose. All rights reserved.

No part of this book may be reproduced, stored in a retrieval system, or transmitted by any means without the written permission of the author.

First published by CrossBooks 6/18/2014

ISBN: 978-1-4627-3736-9 (e)
ISBN: 978-1-4627-3737-6 (sc)

Printed in the United States of America.

This book is printed on acid-free paper.

Certain stock imagery © Thinkstock.
Any people depicted in stock imagery provided by Thinkstock are models, and such images are being used for illustrative purposes only.

All Scripture References are taken from the
New International Version unless otherwise noted

Scripture taken from the Holy Bible, NEW INTERNATIONAL VERSION®. Copyright © 1973, 1978, 1984 by Biblica, Inc. All rights reserved worldwide. Used by permission. NEW INTERNATIONAL VERSION® and NIV® are registered trademarks of Biblica, Inc. Use of either trademark for the offering of goods or services requires the prior written consent of Biblica US, Inc.

Scripture taken from the King James Version of the Bible.

All Scripture quotations in this publications are from The Message. Copyright © by Eugene H. Peterson 1993, 1994, 1995, 1996, 2000, 2001, 2002. Used by permission of NavPress Publishing Group.

Because of the dynamic nature of the Internet, any web addresses or links contained in this book may have changed since publication and may no longer be valid. The views expressed in this work are solely those of the author and do not necessarily reflect the views of the publisher, and the publisher hereby disclaims any responsibility for them.

*"But we have this treasure in jars of clay to show
That this all-surpassing power is
From God and **not from us.**
We are hard pressed on every side, but not crushed;
Perplexed, but not in despair,
Persecuted, but not abandoned;
Struck down, but not destroyed."*

II Corinthians 4:7-9

Acknowledgements

To my precious boys, who have taught me a lot, including how to love selflessly. I will treasure the many wonderful memories we have made together. You are the best gift God has <u>ever</u> given me, and I am thankful every day for you!

To my amazing grandparents, aunts, uncles and cousins, who were the only bright spot in my childhood! Without you, I never would have survived my first 18 years! You believed in me as a child and showed me I was worth something through your words and actions. You are also a gift from God that I will always treasure!

To my church family, who continued to encourage me throughout the writing of this book. It took almost two years to write, and almost another three years to get published, and you helped me keep my dream alive through your words of life and encouragement when I almost gave up on it.

To a very special group of friends, who were with me throughout every season of life and loved me, encouraged me, prayed with me and spoke words of life to me no matter how difficult the valleys were, and were also there to celebrate the greatness of God in my best seasons! My prayer is that God will richly bless you in every way; you have made a huge difference in my life!

Most importantly, I acknowledge the Lord. He has been my everything, and never left my side through thick or thin. Instead, He held me up with His strength, so that I would not be crushed under the weight of all of the difficulties I have faced! I owe Him more than I could ever repay, and there are no words to describe my gratitude for all He has done and continues to do in my life!

Struck Down, But Not Destroyed
(II Corinthians 4:7-9)

Have you been abused? Forgotten? Betrayed? Unemployed? Or, maybe you are fearful of what the future holds? Take heart! God's finest work happens in your weakest moments, when you let Him carry you through the storms of life. He promises to never leave you nor forsake you, especially when life gets tough. He is our restorer, protector, refuge and strength!

Struck Down, But Not Destroyed is a collection of personal testimonies that will inspire and encourage you in the midst of the worst storms in your life. God's strength is made perfect in our weakest moments! He is always alongside you through the deepest valleys and also on the highest mountain tops. The same God who created the universe and placed each star in the sky, naming each one, lovingly records your every lament and collects every tear in His bottle (Psalm 56:8).

Do not allow past mistakes or hurts rob you of the AMAZING life God wants you to experience! I challenge you to desperately seek after Him, love Him with your whole heart, and watch amazing things happen. I promise you, you will NEVER regret it!

*Disclaimer: This is a memoir; my memories as perceived and articulated through my individual experience. Though they are in truth what I experienced, they may not coincide with what others depicted in the story experienced or remember. Therefore, in consideration of that fact and in the interest of protecting identities and privacy, I have changed relationships, names, cities, states and other locations. Any resemblance to actual persons, living or dead, events or locales is entirely coincidental.

I would love to hear how these testimonies have encouraged you or touched your life! Please email me at marie.Rosebook@yahoo.com.

Visit my blog at: www.marierosebook.blogspot.com

Contents

Chapter 1	"Though my mother and father forsake me, the Lord will receive me"	1
Chapter 2	"My Beloved"	13
Chapter 3	Our Honeymoon Years, In the Frigid North	19
Chapter 4	Sanctify Me	28
Chapter 5	Lessons in Forgiveness	36
Chapter 6	Georgia-Bound!	41
Chapter 7	Starting Over With a Promise in Job 8	50
Chapter 8	Thrown Stones	59
Chapter 9	A New Home	66
Chapter 10	Hope Found Amidst a "Hopeless" Situation	72
Chapter 11	YAHWEH ROPHE	84
Chapter 12	A Year of Rest, Blessing and Preparation	99
Chapter 13	The Battle Begins	112
Chapter 14	I am the LORD That Heals You	123
Chapter 15	Growth and Restoration	128

Study Guide	131
Scripture References	141
Endnotes	145

CHAPTER 1

"Though my mother and father forsake me, the Lord will receive me"
(Psalm 27:10)

It was an abusive home; physically, verbally and emotionally. The first memory of mom was that of fear at the young age of three, but not the kind of healthy fear a child has for an adult out of respect for them. This was the kind of fear brought on by being afraid because hurt has already been caused by that person. The next memory of her was when I was five years old. I had come inside from flying my kite on a very windy day and my hair barrette fell out. It was very difficult to put back in myself, so I went inside to ask mom to put it back in for me. When she could not get it to snap back into place either, she lost control of her anger and started pulling my hair so hard I thought she was going to pull it out. Then she went over and totally destroyed my kite in front of me too, which for a child of that age is devastating. After that, I do not have any vivid memories of her for a few years.

Besides the physical abuse, mom was also very controlling. Everything had to be done her way…or watch out. Shower time was limited to five minutes, and when those five minutes were up, she would bang on the door screaming for me to come out. It sure is hard to get clean in five minutes, especially when you are a teenager. She even had a limit imposed on how many toilet paper squares I could use at a time, which was highly unrealistic. I knew by experience to do what I was told, so I did so without argument.

There was also the frequent screaming and being told, in so many words, of my "worthlessness". She implied more than once that surely I would, "not go to heaven because you could not possibly be good enough for that." After moving out of that environment, my eyes were opened for the first time to the fact that these things were far from the truth. It is only by the grace of God and believing that Jesus died for you and having a relationship with Him that gets you to heaven; you don't have to be "good enough" to earn your way there. However, I still struggled for a long time with even believing I was capable of being loved.

Much of my childhood has been blocked from my memory, so I only have a few memories here and there of what happened during those years. I believe that is a blessing! Had I remembered everything, it most likely would have taken a devastating toll on the rest of my life. As **II Corinthians 4:8, 9** says, "We are hard pressed on every side, but not crushed; perplexed, but not in despair, persecuted but not abandoned; struck down, but not destroyed." (NIV) In hind sight, those verses pretty much summed up my life because my childhood did not destroy the rest of my life like it could have easily done. Too many people use their bad childhoods as an excuse for committing crimes or mistreating others when they grow up, thereby, letting their past destroy them.

Dad was never physically abusive, but a workaholic and not around very much; I do not think he even knew about the abuse. I was too scared to tell him or anybody else. I know that he felt he was doing the best thing for us by working hard to provide for us, but kids also need their parents to be there for them and to know they are loved too. I only remember him telling me once during my entire childhood that he loved me.

There was always a feeling of not even being good enough for dad, because he had extremely high standards that could not possibly be met. He often belittled me, which made me feel so ashamed every time I did not do something "right" (his way), to perfection. Eventually I felt ashamed of almost everything I did or said, so I was very shy around other people. I always felt I had done something wrong, even if I had not. Everything, to dad, was seen from a negative viewpoint. Mistakes were unacceptable and not used as teachable moments. Instead, there was shame tied to them.

One time I overheard a conversation between my dad and brother in the basement. My brother felt that dad was always nicer to me than to him, which is normal for a lot of siblings. My dad told him this was because, "I feel like I have to be nicer to her because of how your mother treats her." That was a very difficult thing to hear because I thought that dad was being kinder to me because he thought I was special. Now the truth of the situation was known. I am so glad that my heavenly Father does love me and treat me kindly because I am VERY special to Him and dearly loved for who I am!

As a child, I got a warped sense of who God the Father was in some ways through my childhood experiences with dad. It was very hard believing that my heavenly Father loved me in spite of my imperfections. It truly felt like He was always waiting to punish me and find me guilty of doing something wrong. No matter how hard I tried, I did not think I could ever be good enough to please God or be loved by Him either. I struggled for years with imposing such a high, unachievable standard of perfectionism on myself that could not possibly be reached, hoping that somehow it would make me even the slightest bit loveable to God. I now know, however, that God loves me because He created me and I do not have to "earn" His love.

However, even to this day I occasionally find myself doubting God's love for ME personally because of all I have been through in my life. Deep down, however, I know He does love me because He sent His only son to save me from sin and death, and that is quite a sacrifice to make for somebody whom you do not love. Sometimes I just have to believe that He loves me in *faith* when I go through those times of doubt.

The fact is, we do not have to be perfect or jump through any hoops to earn His love. In fact, we do not have to do anything to earn His love because His nature IS love and He just loves us simply in spite of us, because He created us. We have to be careful not to build our image of who God is and how He relates to us based on our earthly fathers; their love is imperfect, but His love is perfect.

I do, however, have some good memories of my dad, too, because occasionally his fun side came out. He would sometimes rough house with me and my brother, hold us down and tickle us until we could barely breathe, or jump out and "scare" us from around the corner. One good memory in particular was when he took me out to dinner and then dress shopping, telling me I could pick out any dress I wanted. I still remember to this day exactly what that dress looked like; it was powder blue with pinstripes. The collar and sleeves were white. It came just below my knees, and I thought it was the most beautiful dress I had ever seen! I felt like such a princess in it! This was a very special treat because dad was very frugal so he did not spend any money on things that were not absolutely necessary.

Although my dad was not a Christian at the time, he taught me the importance of working hard to earn what I needed and wanted, being honest and living with a strong code of ethics in every area of life, and for this I am very grateful.

There was no feeling of security at home, nor was there at school either. At school I was constantly called names such as "ugly" and ridiculed about the way I looked and dressed, which was not bad; I just had my own style. I was often pushed down, grabbed and teased about everything. Because I was a sensitive child already "beaten down" with such a low self-image from my home life, I was seen as an easy target, the perfect candidate for being bullied and beaten up by the bigger, stronger kids.

Although it was rough at home and at school, I did have a few "safe havens," which were limited to my grandparent's house, my Aunt Bea's house and church. Whenever my mom had to go to the doctor, which was often, I would go to grandma and grandpa's house and we would play games such as Chinese checkers, backgammon, dominoes, trouble and cards. Grandma always let me win. We also made "tents" by draping sheets over the top of cardboard tables. When we were not playing games, we spent a lot of time in the kitchen baking my favorite dessert, Monster cookies. Then we would take walks in the country along the dirt road, picking milkweed and commenting on the cat-tails. I asked her if they were REALLY cat's tails because my dad had jokingly told me they were, and she just chuckled. Even helping grandma do chores like hanging laundry out on the line was always fun.

My grandparents lived on a farm so there were always a lot of fun things to do and explore outside when we were not playing games or baking cookies. When I stayed overnight, grandma always woke me up by pulling the cover off of my face and saying, "somebody is playing possum" and chuckle as she walked away. Grandpa always got a kick out of poking me with his cane, teasing me in a funny way or tossing a pillow at me, and his deep-bellied laugh was very contagious! There were so many happy memories at their house, and I always looked forward to going there because I felt secure…and I could have carefree fun just being a kid.

My Aunt Bea's house was also a lot of fun, because they also lived on a farm so there was always a lot to explore and do around there too. My oldest cousin and I would jump between the large bales of straw out in the field and see who could make it the fastest down the line. We also played house in a real child-sized two story "house" my uncle built in her playroom. Even though my aunt was quite strict, I knew she cared about me and believed the best in me by the positive words she spoke to me. Sometimes she made us work very hard hoeing the garden until we developed blisters, but she would also sometimes reward us by taking us out for ice cream, which made it worthwhile for a kid.

I always felt the Holy Spirit's presence in Aunt Bea's home the minute I arrived. Often I would ask to go over to her house on Sundays after church, as Sundays were always the worst day with mom. I know there were times my cousin was tired of me always asking to come over after church, but she did not realize the nightmare I was living through at home and how much opening her home ministered to me.

On Sunday mornings, my Aunt Essie taught my Sunday school class and I always looked forward to going there, too. I found comfort in the Bible stories I learned about, in the fun songs we sang and in the kindness shown to me by Aunt Essie and many others at church. She really had great enthusiasm for teaching children and it showed in how she interacted with us.

I also have fond memories of family gatherings at my grandparent's house when all six of us grandkids, who lived within fifteen minutes of each other, would get together. One of the things we really liked to do was explore the barn and climb down the ladder into the silo. We also really enjoyed climbing on the straw bales stacked up high in the barn and looking for owl's nests.

One of my personal favorite activities at those gatherings was using a small inflatable kid-sized pool as a boat and a stick as an oar to row us across the giant water puddles that would stay around for days after a big rainfall. I wished I could have stayed there every day because it was like a fun escape from what I had to endure every day at home and school.

Besides having wonderful grandparents and aunts, I was graciously blessed with a dog to comfort me and show me unconditional love during my childhood. I believe that God used my dog to help me stay strong enough to get through the hardest childhood moments when I felt like giving up. I was a sensitive child who had a big heart for animals, especially dogs.

Through the good times and bad, I always remember having a strong faith in God as a child and believing that He was always there somewhere. I did not question or doubt the Bible, but believed it with childlike faith. This faith in God was my biggest "safe haven," so to speak. The only thing I really ever struggled believing about God was His unconditional love for ME. I always heard about His love in Sunday school, but found it so hard to truly believe in my heart because I did not feel loved by my parents. If they did not even love me (and parents are "supposed to,") then how or why would God love me or find value in me? Also, why would He allow this daily nightmare (called my life) to go on day after day and not even help it get better?

Going into my teen years, the abuse seemed to get more frequent and I was often at the mercy of mom's anger and rage. She would be fine one minute and the next she would fly into a rage, grab the closest object next to her, and hit me with it. Sometimes out of anger she would tear up the house looking for something, which always scared me, and then scream at me to come and clean it all up after her. Looking back, I know that the protective hand of God was over me.

Throughout my teen years, I struggled with depression. Part of this was also due to genetic inheritance as there was a history of some depression on both sides of my family. However, some of it was also due to the difficult life I had both at home and school.

I also struggled constantly with a very low self-image. It was almost impossible for me to look at people in the face when talking to them. I was fearful of most people because I did not trust them or believe they thought there was anything good about me. All I knew was that in many cases people hurt me and treated me as if I were a worthless throw-away. I occasionally talked to the high school counselor when things got really bad, which helped a little, and I often wrote my feelings and thoughts in a journal because I really enjoyed writing. I also wrote many poems as an outlet for my emotions. Although these were all important things to help me cope, I did not fully heal until I moved out and was completely away from that home and school environment.

My situation at home and school along with the depression got to the point that I did not even want to live anymore. Many times I felt like Job did in the Bible, and it seemed that those people who should have been there for me to help me through this were not helping me but only making things more difficult. Many times it felt like God was nowhere around either. Nightmares were common, and a recurring nightmare in particular haunted me the most. Somebody was always chasing me in the woods at night trying to kill me, and I was fearfully running for my life trying to save it from this unknown person. Yet, during the day I did not want to live. Though my dreams seemed conflicting to how I felt in real life, they seemed to be a continuation of the nightmare I lived during the day.

Twice during my teen years I took a bottle full of various pills I found throughout the house hoping it would numb me or end the pain for good, but by the grace of God, I vomited them up both times and I was not brave enough to try to end my life any other way. By then I knew I was not going to be successful in taking my own life, so I asked God to take me out of this life somehow.

The bullying and ridicule I faced seemed worse in my teen years. I had a few close friends, but many of the kids were cruel, as kids can be. One time in particular when I was coming out of the shower after gym class, a bunch of girls turned around, looked at me and sang the "jello song," which was a popular song on a television commercial at the time. This was because they thought I jiggled like jello due to being a little overweight. When looking back at pictures of myself at that age, I do not think I was fat at all and wish

I could only be that thin again. However, I always felt like I was as big as a whale because of what everybody told me all the time. My perception of myself was distorted, and this too took several years to overcome.

That is only one example of many difficult moments I had while going through school. Looking back, I can only imagine how sad Jesus must have felt to see one of His beloved children being treated that way. However, God can even use what somebody else meant for evil and turn it into good down the road, just like He did for Joseph in the Bible. Initially, his brothers were going to kill him and tell their father a wild animal had taken Joseph's life. Then after their brother Reuben intervened, they decided to throw him into a cistern instead and leave him for dead. Their plan changed when some merchants came by, and they agreed to take him out of the cistern and sell him into slavery. He was later accused of something he did not do and unjustly thrown into prison. However, he later became somebody great and powerful. (Genesis 37, 39)

When I hit rock-bottom and had nowhere else to turn, I decided to start devoting more time to praying and reading the Bible more regularly. This is what usually happens with most people; they do not fully turn to God until things hit rock-bottom. God's Word was there all along ready to give me encouragement and hope, but I actually had to take the time to read it and meditate on it to get the full benefit from it. Reading the scriptures on my own brought some comfort and enjoyment. I found that the more I prayed and read the Bible, the closer I felt to God and the more peaceful and comforted I felt even through the storms I was facing throughout my teenage years.

I enjoyed reading the Psalms the most. I still remember the first time I read **Psalm 27:10** which says, "Though my mother and father forsake me, the LORD will receive me." (NIV) Right there, it said to me that God DID in fact love and accept me, whether or not my parents did.

Shortly after finding that verse, I decided to read the Bible from beginning to end to see what other gems of encouragement and hope I could find. This was the only thing that helped me bear the last few years at home. No, my situation did not change a whole lot for the better, but it was easier to get through each day knowing that God was by my side. He spoke to my heart through the verses on those pages and I was very grateful and excited about it. His Word was one of my only sources of hope, peace and strength to make it through another day. **Psalm 119:92** says, "If your law had not been my delight, I would have perished in my affliction." (NIV) I know that I would not have survived what I went through as a child as well as I did without His Word becoming my delight.

God promises us in His Word that He will restore our lives and give us comfort and peace through our difficult moments. He will not "leave us nor forsake us," especially when we are striving to live for Him.

It's amazing how different people see and react to bad life experiences in one of two ways. Either they blame God for their bad situation and turn away from Him in anger, OR they draw close to God and have the blessed opportunity to fully experience His unconditional love and special protection, which helps them make it through and come out stronger. The ONLY way I even survived my childhood and have come through it as well as I have is because I chose to draw closer to God. I also had His hand of mercy and protection over me in more ways than I even knew at the time.

When I was sixteen years old, I was in a serious car accident. It was again by the grace of God I even survived. I was in the front passenger seat and we were hit directly on my side of the car. Though my seat was smashed down to only half of its original size, I managed to escape with only internal injuries and several large facial cuts needing almost twenty stitches. Later, I was told that had I not been wearing my seatbelt, I would have been ejected from the car and not survived.

As I was in bed recuperating from the accident, I realized just how fortunate I was to survive. The Lord showed me through that accident how much He did love me and that He had a purpose for my life. It was a big wake-up call for me to the fact that I was still alive for a reason and that my life was a precious gift. In a way, I was trying to "play God" by attempting to take my own life, the life He gave me, before it was my time. At that moment I was filled with regret for having had those suicidal intentions. Because of that accident, I rededicated my life to the Lord.

I have **not** had another single episode of depression since that accident, and I believe that God miraculously healed my depression and emotional wounds in a way that only He could! I *could* have undergone counseling for years and struggled my way through, but I believe that the Lord gave me an even better outcome and future than what any professional counselor could have given me. He has truly been my, "Wonderful Counselor, Almighty God, Everlasting Father, and [my] Prince of Peace!" (Isaiah 9:6)

That was a turning point in my faith. A few years later, when I was eighteen, I enrolled at a Christian college close to home. Although it was only thirty minutes away from home, I chose to live on campus. I needed to have space to let the wounds heal from my childhood. Just as importantly, I had to work on forgiving my parents and the others who had hurt me so much as a child. Those four years were a time of great growth in my personal and spiritual life. Yes, I had several issues to work through with forgiveness and low self-esteem, but I also thrived and learned how to love others as well as accept being loved by them.

A whole new world opened up for me in college. I made lots of friends and found that I really enjoyed social activities. I opened up a lot and began to learn to accept myself for who I was. God brought several special friends into my life to be a source of new strength and comfort for me. Through them I was able to see that I was somebody special. It was like starting over with a clean slate.

Although college life was a lot of fun, I still had to work out this whole forgiveness thing, particularly with mom. She wrote me a long letter after the first few weeks of being away at school, saying that she missed me and that "maybe [she] was a little too hard on [me] but [she] just wanted [me] to turn out right." I suppose that was her way of apologizing to me. However, I already knew that it was not her iron fist that made me turn out right, but only what God did in my life. Perhaps it was also my determination to make something good out of my life and to rise above my bad childhood.

I'll be honest. It took a long time and was a huge step for me, but I was finally able to forgive everybody from my childhood who mistreated me. It took a lot of conscious effort and prayer on my part along with the Lord's encouragement and grace. It was possible to have the victory over this situation and not allow those who mistreated me to reign victorious!

In my 20s, I realized that mom had some emotional issues along with depression caused by some very difficult trials that she faced, which I did not know about until years later. To a certain extent, her behavior may have been beyond her control. Truthfully, she probably did not even realize that most of what she was doing or saying was as harmful as it actually was. She did not have the ability to sympathize or empathize with others at all. Although she is better now, she still has some of those issues, and all I can do is pray for her and choose to love and honor her anyway, because she is still my mother.

Normally, it is the case when someone hurts us deeply that they either do not realize the damage they caused or they get over it amazingly fast. They move on with their lives without a second thought. The problem with not forgiving them and holding onto the anger and hurt is that it will eventually destroy you, and only you, while they go on merrily with their lives. There is great power and healing in letting go of it and letting God be the one to deal with those who have hurt us. We will all be held accountable some day for how we treated others, and there will be a Day of Judgment and punishment. We need to trust that it will all be taken care of in the end by a just, perfect God.

God's Word says that He is our refuge, strength, comforter, deliverer, restorer, hope and help! He wants more than anything else to save us, and as Christians give us hope, restore us and give us abundant life. He does not want our past to hold us down and take control over our lives, nor does he want us to live in bitterness and unforgiveness. That is what Satan wants for us.

I am not saying, however, it was easy because I had to spend a lot of time on my knees asking God to help me and give me the strength and ability to forgive those who hurt me all those years. I also had to consciously and deliberately work at seeing myself as God saw me, a wonderful and precious creation, not as others saw me. That was a necessary part of the healing process in order for me to ever move on and live the abundant life God wanted for me.

There are still times even today when I feel very unattractive physically. Again, I have to remind myself it does not matter what I look like or what others think of me but only what God thinks of me. By the grace of God, it is almost as if most of the damaging things in my childhood never happened! I was given the gift of a clean slate to start over. My life has taken a complete 180-degree turn from what it was back then. I give the Lord ALL the glory and praise for what He helped me overcome and how He has made something good out of my life despite the very rough start I had!

I have realized over the past twenty-five years what wonderful blessings I would have missed out on had my life ended as I wanted it to in my teen years. He WAS right…there was a special purpose for my life! ~**Amen**

CHAPTER 2

"My Beloved"

When I was eighteen years old, I went to a small, Christian liberal arts college about twenty-five miles from home; far enough to get away yet close enough to my extended family to be able to visit occasionally. I was so excited to see what life was like outside of the environment I grew up in, and looking forward to my newfound independence.

I found that I enjoyed my classes in the sciences, so I was planning on earning a Biology degree and eventually going into the medical technology field. I also took Spanish because I really enjoyed it in high school and wanted to continue perfecting this skill. Besides the excitement of getting to choose the classes I wanted to take, I signed up for several social events as well.

I quickly found out that things were completely different in college. I was not very popular in high school and was teased…a LOT. The guys wanted nothing to do with me in high school, so I never experienced going to junior or senior prom. Needless to say, I was anything but confident in myself at the time.

However, something amazing and exciting happened very soon after I started college. I found myself making friends quickly and enjoyed going out with them. I was also being asked out by the guys for the first time. I was quite puzzled because I did not know how things could have changed so much in one summer, between my senior year in high school and my freshman year in college. For the most part, it seemed like everybody matured overnight and the taunts and teases were traded instead for friendship and maturity. All I knew was that for the first time in my life, I began to see that life wasn't so bad and I wasn't as bad as I had been led to believe all those years growing up. I started gaining confidence in myself and began doing things I had never done before. My social calendar was filling up fast, though I did make sure my studies were top priority. I wanted to do well in my classes too, and I had to work very hard to achieve good grades.

My first year was a lot of fun, though uneventful for the most part. It was the best year of my life up to that point. In my second year of college, I met new people and had new roommates, two of whom occasionally enjoyed a few drinks here and there, especially on weekends. I went to a few parties and even got drunk one time, but found out quickly that this type of lifestyle was not one that I enjoyed at all. I still managed to do fairly well in my classes and dated a few guys here and there. Later on that year, I met and enjoyed spending more time with a new group of strong Christian friends, who helped me stay on the right road in my Christian walk.

The summer after my sophomore year, I decided to go on a mission's trip to Nicaragua. I first heard about this opportunity in my advanced Spanish course. I never did anything like that before but I could speak Spanish quite well by that point and I really enjoyed travelling. After some prayer, I talked to my dad about it and asked if he would pay for me to go. It was going to be an expensive trip and knowing how much my dad hated to spend any money, I was not sure he would even agree to it. Also, he was not a Christian at the time so I was almost certain he would not support me financially to go on a summer-long mission's trip. However, I found out that when the Lord wants you to do something, He will always make a way for it to happen, and my dad agreed to send me.

When the time came for me to go, I got on a plane for the first time in my life and flew thousands of miles to Nicaragua. I boarded the plane with another student from my college whom I had not met until this trip. We were going to be roommates once we got there. We very quickly became close friends. My Spanish language ability was much more advanced than hers; I had studied Spanish for five years by that time and she for only a year, so she depended on my language ability to help her communicate with the natives. Once we arrived in Nicaragua, we were tested and placed into intensive language courses where we would learn the language and cultural skills necessary to work in the local churches effectively. We were also placed into sponsor's homes, where we would be totally immersed in this new language and culture.

Along with language classes, we helped lead worship in our local Spanish-speaking church each Sunday and taught Vacation Bible School in some of the outlying villages during the week. We also learned skits and children's songs in Spanish that we could take out to the community to introduce Christ to children in a fun way. A few times we even went door-to-door bringing the gospel message to the community, which was about 90% Roman Catholic. We had the opportunity to lead a revival service in Spanish and each was given a special job to do according to interests and Spanish-speaking ability. It was so touching to see how loving and receptive the people were to hearing about God's love and how grateful they were that we were there giving of our time.

One day when we went evangelizing door-to-door, a young lady of about fifteen years of age answered our knock. She invited us in, and we started to form a friendship with her. We agreed to come back again, but before we did, we prayed for her and for our words to be what she needed to hear. That next time we went back and spoke to her, I amazingly started to recite Scripture after Scripture in Spanish that I had not yet memorized. After we left this young lady's house, I turned to my roommate and said, "I do not even remember which Scriptures I quoted, nor do I know where all of that came from, because it wasn't from me!" Of course, I really knew it was the Lord speaking through me to share those particular Scriptures she needed to hear. That is the only explanation for so many Scriptures pouring out, one after the other, more quickly than I could even think about what I was saying.

We worked very long, hard hours but also had opportunities to sitesee. Every day we took "El Metro" (the subway) to and from classes and also to visit some of the sites. One time in particular, my roommate and I had been on the subway crammed in like sardines when a guy in front of me reached back and grabbed ahold of my wrist. I tried to get it away from him but the harder I pulled, the harder he held on to me. I was afraid he was going to pull me off of the subway at the next stop and that I might then be unable to get away from him. I did the only thing I could think of doing, which was what our advisors told us to do if we ever got in a situation like this. I hollered out as loud as I could, "Dejame, grosero!!" (Let go of me, you pig!!); it worked! I hit him on the shoulder hard with my other hand and he let go immediately. To do something like that is totally out of character for me, but because I felt I was in a dangerous situation, my "fight or flight" response kicked in. Apparently, it is a common problem down there. Though it was scary at the moment, it was funny later on. That was one of several times the Lord protected me while in Nicaragua.

Between all the people I met and the family with whom I lived, I really fell in love with the Nicaraguan people. They were far more giving than many Americans and often gave sacrificially to us. Our "hermano" (brother) would take my roommate and me to get cokes to drink, usually with his last few coins, when he met us to walk us home. If he did not have enough for himself, he would always make sure that at the very least, we got something to drink on that long, hot walk back to the house.

Most Nicaraguans have very close-knit families, and after a few weeks we met the whole extended family too. There was one cousin in particular named Eduardo, who seemed to have an interest in me. He went to the church we were working in, and I started to see him regularly between church and family time. It took several times of him coming to the house for me to even realize he was interested in me, because that was absolutely the last thing on my mind while I was there. The last month I was there, he asked me out on a date. Although I had no interest in dating anybody while I was there, we went out a few times before I left Nicaragua in between language classes, mission work, sightseeing and time with our adoptive family.

I learned quickly that in their culture, the guy asks a girl on a date after he first gets to know you a little. That first date is very important because the man comes right out and asks if the girl will be his girlfriend…no games, no hidden agenda…either yes or no. Eduardo was a very smart, nice looking, good Christian man who had a great, close family, which was another attraction to me because I did not have that. I did keep my main focus on the real reason I was there in the first place, but this made the summer even more special. I loved the work I did while in Nicaragua and my faith in God grew; I matured a great deal spiritually and emotionally throughout that summer.

When I flew back home after the summer was over, I saw things differently than before. People were much more important to me and I learned to be more selfless by sacrificially giving to others. Whenever I got tempted to keep for myself what I knew someone else could use, I would think back to how much those people gave to me out of what little they had, and gladly gave up what I had to give to others.

A few weeks after returning, I started my junior year of college. I was looking forward to what this brand new year had in store for me. I grew a little more confident and even more spiritually and emotionally throughout that year. I still kept in contact with Eduardo by letter and phone and we visited each other when we could. I developed excellent Spanish-speaking skills through all of this, for he did not speak English. We continued dating through the following summer, and things were going in a more serious direction…towards marriage.

Because he lived so far away, I seriously started praying about this relationship and the direction it was going in because I wanted to be sure he was the right one for me. I knew that once we got married, I would either have to move thousands of miles away or he would have to move here which would be a difficult transition, especially for the one moving. I am the type of person who puts my all into everything. I love hard, play hard, work hard and study hard. For this reason, I wanted to be sure this was what God wanted for me before I put everything into it.

Shortly after I started praying seriously about this relationship, I began to wake up in the middle of the night out of a deep sleep. A feeling of sudden, intense fear about this relationship would grip me at that time; I just knew that he was not the right man for me and I needed to break it off. Part of me was sad about it because I really loved this man and things were going well between us. I was convinced, however, that it was God speaking to me. The time came when I had to make that phone call to tell him I could no longer date him. I told him I had prayed about it and felt it was not right. There was just a long silence on the other end of the phone; he was devastated to hear that news. We both fell in love hard; as my roommate told me, we were like "two lovesick cows mooing in the pasture."

For many reasons, that was the hardest thing I ever had to do up to that point in my life. Even though it was a very difficult decision to make, a huge burden was lifted and I felt so much better after the initial sadness of breaking off that relationship.

I still sometimes wonder how my life would have been with Eduardo and why God was so persistent in keeping this relationship from going to marriage. He was my first true love and special to me for that reason. I may never know the reason, but only God can see the future and, quite possibly, He saved me from what could have been a very difficult life ahead. I only know that I was obedient to something I knew the Lord wanted me to do, and I was at peace about it afterwards.

About a month later, I met Jake, a new transfer student...

CHAPTER 3

Our Honeymoon Years, In the Frigid North

Jake and I dated for six months before we were convinced that we were meant for each other. During my senior year in college, we were inseparable. We had so much fun together and enjoyed taking long walks downtown at night and going to baseball games, concerts and the symphony.

Because my parents lived close to my school, they had the opportunity to meet Jake and see him occasionally. They, of course, fell in love with him as did the rest of my extended family. I remember early on in our relationship when I was at my grandma's house and she said my first name with his last name. She chuckled and said that those names sounded good together. I was close to my grandparents, so it was a special deal for her to comment about my new relationship.

When Jake asked my dad for my hand in marriage, my dad thought very highly of that gesture because many guys were no longer traditional in that sense. He told Jake to make sure he treated me right because I had gone through a difficult childhood. Dad wanted to be sure that I would well taken care of by my new husband. After their conversation, I was quite eager to see when I would get the ring because the proposal date was still a surprise.

That summer, Jake and I took a road trip to his home town, which was out of state. He ended up proposing to me there at a local park on a beautiful lake. After he got down on his knee and proposed to me (again, as was tradition and something I loved), he told me that he had kept the ring hidden inside the glove box of the same car we had taken on this road trip. Even though I had opened up the glove box several times during our trip, I never even saw it! I am glad for that because it would have ruined the very special surprise he had in store for me. He had music playing, the whole nine yards. It was quite romantic, the picture of perfection!

We were engaged for an entire year before getting married. I was so madly in love with Jake. I thought I had found the perfect man, and I truly had him up on a pedestal. Of course, when one is so deeply in love, blinders tend to hide flaws of all sorts, and even some potential red flags are not clearly seen. I did pray about this relationship some, but it was something I wanted so badly that I did not really take the time and attention needed to hear what God had to say about it. Had I really taken time to prayerfully consider this, I do not think it would have gone to marriage in the first place. I would pray a little and then say to God, "please, please, please let Jake be the right one...," but not even wait or listen for His response in the matter.

The big day had finally arrived! After preparing for a full year, I was very excited about the special day finally being here! It was such a beautiful wedding and fun, too. A little humor was mixed in to make the day even more enjoyable. Jake dropped the ring when he first took it from the best man, and then dipped me during "the kiss" in such a manner that my veil almost fell off. Then to top that off, the minister left out the best song from the ceremony that I had my heart most set on. In the end, that did not matter though because it was still a magical day.

Afterwards, we headed downtown to the nicest hotel in the city. I had won a free honeymoon suite in this particular hotel at a bridal fair I had attended a few months prior to our wedding. I had never won anything before, which made it even more special. We then flew to Hawaii and spent a week there. I love to travel and had traveled quite a bit growing up but had never been to Hawaii before, so Jake thought this would be a great new location to visit for our honeymoon.

The first few years were great! Everyone had always told me that the first year of marriage was the toughest, but our first year was overall more wonderful than I even imagined it would be!

When Jake graduated, he got a job that would require us to move to the far northwestern part of the country. Not really anything to get excited about, especially with the long, hard winters and seclusion it had to offer. I knew that God MUST have a sense of humor to have allowed us to, out of all the other company locations, be put into such a cold, snowy, secluded… and did I mention no city-in-sight-for-shopping-pleasure, place. However, the good thing that came out of it was that the Lord broke me from the bondage of materialism by having me live in such a secluded location. I learned that I could live without a lot of material things and still be happy!

Being the traveler that I am and the love I have for doing new and exciting things, I thought I would make the best of it; it would not be forever anyway, or at least I hoped not! Besides, I had agreed to support my husband no matter where his job took us. Another drawback was that it was about 3,000 miles away from our families and friends. Previously, I had never lived outside of my home state nor lived too far away from a big city.

Soon after we got the go-ahead from his company, we loaded up the car. Jake and I joked that we looked like a traveling circus with our car piled high with many of our belongings. We then began our long drive northwestward.

We made a vacation out of the drive, sightseeing all the way to our destination. That part of the country was more beautiful than I had ever imagined! Everyone we met joked with us when we arrived after this very long, cross-country drive by asking, "and you are still married??!" We actually had a very enjoyable trip and saw a lot of things along the way, including wildlife I had never seen before in my part of the country.

After we arrived at our destination and got settled into a rental house, I was taking our dog on a walk. I saw a moose just up ahead of me standing in a swamp next to the road on which I was walking. I very quietly stood still and watched to see what the moose would do when he saw me. I thought that maybe I could slowly back up and walk away without being detected. My plan almost worked, until my dog saw the moose and it was ON! He started barking like crazy, and then the moose saw us and started his way out of the swamp towards the hill, running towards us. I turned and ran so fast in the opposite direction that my dog, still on the leash, could barely keep up. I was literally dragging the poor thing on the ground for a short distance. I was unsure at the time whether or not the moose was close behind me and unaware of the fact that I never could have outrun the moose anyway. I just wanted to get home safely with my dog and myself in one piece.

When I was almost home, I turned around and looked, but the moose had bluffed me. He had apparently crossed the road I had been on and went down into the swamp on the other side of the road. Needless to say, it was some time before I ventured out on that same path with my dog again. Right around the corner from my house, I started to slow down to a walking speed again after I realized the moose was gone. A neighbor then yelled out her window at me to get my dog off her lawn. Apparently, I had broken a cardinal rule by allowing his paws to touch the very edge of her lawn. (I was a little preoccupied at the time to even notice).

When I got home, I was so overwhelmed emotionally between being chased by the moose and then yelled at by a new neighbor that I kept crying and could not stop. Even though I knew I was usually sensitive to things like this, it still hit me as odd because I normally got over things fairly quickly, but this time I literally could not stop myself from crying.

Soon after, I found out I was pregnant with our first child. That explained the uncontrollable crying…pregnancy hormones. I was very excited about finally being pregnant because we had tried unsuccessfully for four months! I was ready and looking forward to being a mother. However, it did not seem like my husband was quite as elated as I was about it, but I reasoned that it was just a "guy thing." Even though I wished he had shared more in my excitement, I was still so deeply in love with him that I did not make a big deal over this. Plus, the excitement (and sickness) that pregnancy brought kept my mind occupied.

About two months into the pregnancy, I started bleeding heavily. I thought I was having a miscarriage, so my husband took me to the local hospital where they did an ultrasound. Thankfully, everything still looked normal. The doctor did say though that he could not guarantee I would carry this pregnancy to term. It was a waiting game at that point. I was very thankful to the Lord when I went to my next OB appointment and my doctor said that everything looked good and the heartbeat was still strong. I already knew I had a fighter in there, and I was right.

About five months into my pregnancy, I flew home by myself to see my family. My mom and grandma had a surprise baby shower for me. It was very special because a lot of my extended family and friends from the church I had attended as a teenager were there to celebrate with me. It was a great feeling seeing my mom so excited about having her first grandchild on the way! Although we still were not really close, this pregnancy brought us closer together. She showed me more love and attention during those nine months than in my entire childhood. She practically bought out every baby store in the state. This baby was not going to lack ANYTHING having her as a grandma!

One of those days while I was back home, we were going into town when my dad rear-ended the car in front of us. I was again worried about the baby I was carrying although I felt perfectly fine besides being shaken up. Because everybody appeared to be fine, the police told me to go to the hospital if I started cramping or bleeding to get checked out. Fortunately, I had no physical problems after that accident. When we hit the car in front of us, even the baby jumped inside of me like he was putting on the brakes too. It was actually very cute! Another pregnancy scare at the moment, but I later felt the baby moving normally, so I thanked the Lord again for His protection on me and my baby.

Near the end of my pregnancy, I was quite clumsy and fell down the stairs. Another time I slipped and fell on the ice while taking my daily walk around the neighborhood. Fortunately, I was able to catch myself both times with my arms to prevent my stomach from hitting the ground or ice full force. I only had a few scratches and everything else appeared to be fine, except for my pride. I went to see my doctor after the second fall just to be sure all was still going well. Again, the heartbeat was strong. I really felt that God had a special purpose for this child to get him through all of this even before he was born.

The time came for Joshua to be born, and it was a very long and painful twenty-eight hours of hard back labor to get him here. I immediately fell in love with all 9 pounds of him. He was so beautiful that my heart melted whenever I looked into those precious blue eyes. Although he was very adorable to look at, he cried…a LOT. I asked the nurse around five o'clock that morning to take him back to the nursery so I could get at least a few hours of sleep. When the nurse brought him back to me a few hours later she said, "He's going to be handful," for he cried the entire time, very loudly. I guess he just wanted his mama!

Some guy was at the hospital visiting another lady who had just given birth and said something to me about "having a quiver full of children." Of course, I knew that my child was a huge blessing from God but after the past 30+ hours of all the physical demands my body just had forced upon it coupled with the lack of sleep for the past two nights did not make it well received at that very moment.

The nurse was right, by the way, for during the first year of Joshua's life we were tested beyond our limits with a high-needs (but extremely cute) new bundle of joy. He constantly cried, ate a lot and never slept for more than a few minutes at a time the whole first year of his life. I took him to the pediatrician several times convinced something was very wrong with him, but they assured me he appeared healthy and just had a bad case of colic. I was overwhelmed being at home all day long and all he did was cry, no matter what I did to try to soothe him. This made it harder for me to enjoy his first year. I tried every single recommendation from the pediatrician and from family and friends, but nothing worked.

Why didn't anybody else's baby behave this way? What was wrong with me? Was I just a bad mother, unable to keep my baby happy? Although I loved him more than life itself, sometimes I needed to put him safely in his crib, close the door and go outside on the front porch for a while to allow him to have his cry fest and for me to get a grip on my sanity. Every night, I took a thirty-minute walk alone to collect my thoughts and relax in quiet by letting daddy take over for a bit when he came home.

Usually, Jake was good about giving me an occasional break when I needed one, which helped a lot. I thought maybe it was something I was doing wrong, but daddy could not get him to stay quiet and content either. There were many nights when Jake or I would have to take a drive so Joshua could fall asleep in the car. It would work for a while but the minute we took him out of the car, he would wake up again and start crying again. We tried the whole let-him-cry-himself-to-sleep bit, but after an hour-and-a-half of screaming, he was just getting warmed up!

During this stressful year with our high-needs baby, I started to notice that my husband was being dishonest, even about little things. I was naïve up to this point because I fully trusted him. I thought that because I had always been fully honest with him about everything (sometimes too honest), that surely he would be the same. For instance, when I had to leave the house and would call in to check on Joshua, Jake said he had already fed him his baby food. However, when I got home the baby food, spoon and bib would still be on the counter untouched. Jake would respond that he just gave Joshua his bottle.

My sense of trust began to decline after several instances because he was not only untruthful about the small things, but also about bigger things. I began to see a pattern develop; he would have to lie to cover up lies already told and then sometimes forget what he had said originally. Although this really bothered me a lot, I was too busy taking care of Joshua to worry much about it.

Around a year old, Joshua began to sleep half the night and then soon afterwards the entire night. I could finally start taking him to the grocery store without him screaming the entire time. Looking back, I think he was just bored and constantly had to be engaged in everything to keep his little mind occupied. Joshua developed skills far earlier than most babies his age, including walking and talking very early. This also meant that he got into a lot of things far earlier than other babies and had to be constantly watched. My favorite thing to watch him do when he was about a year old was that he would go around the house, collect all similar toys and line them up in a perfectly straight line. For some reason, that kept him occupied for quite a while.

For his first birthday, I had a huge birthday party in which we had a houseful of guests and enough food to feed an army. It was actually two parties in one; one party to celebrate Joshua's birth date and another party to celebrate the fact we made it through the challenging first year!

Although Joshua was a very difficult baby the first year, after he turned one year old he became the most enjoyable toddler! He was a very busy little guy, full of smiles, always getting into everything and climbing over everything he could find. He was so much fun to have around! He was already beginning to talk in three and four-word sentences, and his little personality started coming out. I started to bond with him more at that age. Maybe having one more in our quiver would be a good thing after all!

When Joshua started sleeping through most of the night, Jake would get up with him and try to help him back to sleep on the weekends to give me a break from getting up so much. One night in particular I heard Joshua cry, but when I rolled over to wake up Jake, he was gone. I checked downstairs to see where he was, but everything was dark. I went in to get Joshua and after putting him back into bed, I checked the driveway for the car but it was gone. I wondered where he could possibly be in the middle of the night, as we lived in the middle of nowhere. There was not much entertainment going on during the night hours where we lived. They pretty much rolled up the sidewalks by 9:00 p.m.

The next day, Jake said that he went into work in the middle of the night to finish up some things he needed to do. It was out of character for him to go in after office hours to work. It felt like he was being sneaky, and I did not know if I could even believe he actually went into work at that hour. Although it was hard to do, I said my peace and then let it go because I was so tired all the time. I needed to use my energy to focus on the baby and rest when I could. It did not even seem worth the argument.

While all of this was going on, a close friend of mine began making comments about how fortunate I was to be married to Jake. One day she called, as she did every single day, to talk about baby things as she had a daughter very close to my son's age; however this time she asked if Jake was home. I thought that this was very odd because she had never asked for him before. I told her that Jake was at work, and she said to have him call her when he got home. I asked if I could give him a message and she said, "No."

When Jake got come, I told him she had called so he returned her call. He told me that she had invited him to go the fair with her…just him and her. She did not ask all of us to go, nor did she mention her husband going. What a slap in the face! I trusted her up to that point and thought we were good friends. Our friendship was never the same after that. Not only was I losing trust in my husband, whom I still loved, (but was beginning not to like so much) I was now facing trust issues with someone that I thought was a good friend. She had even been in the delivery room with me when I gave birth to my son.

Although my husband and I started to have trust issues, we still had some good times here and there. For our anniversary, we took a train trip. It was nice to get away as a couple again, which we had not done since Joshua was born. After taking the train through the beautiful mountains, we stayed overnight in a lodge. The view was breathtaking! We also had some much needed quiet time to reconnect and have fun together in a different setting.

Nine months later, David came along, and he was a joy from the very beginning! I even nudged him in his bassinet a few times at the hospital because he slept so much that I thought surely he had stopped breathing. He even slept well at night too. He was a very easy-going baby. We were not expecting to have another baby so close in age to our oldest child. That first year of Joshua's life we considered not another child because of the challenges we faced the first time around. However, when Joshua was just over a year old, God had other plans for us, and I am grateful He blessed us twice!

When baby David was only three months old, my husband's company relocated him so we had to pack up and move. I was glad to be leaving the frigid North for the most part because I was so tired of seeing so much snow every year. I was ready to defrost for good. However, I made a lot of great, lasting friendships and saw a lot of beautiful things I knew I would never see again. Overall it was a good experience. On the way to the airport, a moose and her two babies walked out in front of our car as the sun was rising. It was a beautiful sight I will never forget! I cried at that point knowing I would never again see such beauty. It was truly a bittersweet moment. What a wonderful memory God gave me to cherish as we closed out some very interesting and difficult few years.

> *"Sons are a heritage from the LORD,*
> *Children a reward from him."*
> **Psalm 127:3 (NIV)**

Chapter 4

Sanctify Me

We all made the very long flight to our next destination where our new home would be. It took roughly thirteen hours, which was no easy task...traveling with a three-month-old, a very active two-year-old and a hyper dog.

When we arrived, we began shopping for a bigger vehicle. We opted for a large car, which was the perfect choice for a growing family. Besides a new vehicle, we also had to begin looking for a house. In the meantime, we had to stay in a small hotel room, which offered very little living space. Although it was cramped quarters and very stressful, I knew that we would find a house soon so I tried to make the best of it. Besides, our belongings would not be there for a while yet any way.

It took over a month, but when we finally moved into a house, it was an exciting day! Although our belongings had not made it to us yet, the boys each had their own bedroom and even a playroom. Although the house was older than and not nearly as nice as the rental we had previously, the neighborhood was much bigger and we were surrounded by lots of neighbors. There was even a playground right around the corner from our house. I could not wait to meet our neighbors!

A few weeks later, our belongings arrived. It was like Christmas getting to unwrap all of our household belongings. I enjoyed setting up and decorating our new home. It was very challenging getting all of the boxes unpacked and everything put away with a baby, a toddler and a hyper dog. Right after our shipment arrived, my husband had to go out of town for business so I was left alone for the week to get the house in order. I could only do a little bit each day due to my other responsibilities, but I worked very hard at trying to get as much done as I could so that the necessities were easily available to me. I first unpacked the cooking supplies and kid's belongings.

As I was unpacking the kitchen boxes my toddler, being the very curious and "helpful" child he was (as any toddler can be), took a piece of stemmed glassware (from a set of two, mind you) out of a box to hand to me. As he unwrapped the paper from around it…crash! It fell to the floor. I could not help but laugh because I thought, "that glass made it all the way here from across the country without a single scratch, but then ends up shattered into a thousand pieces after finally getting here!"

Despite the setbacks, I thought I did a good job at getting things unpacked and in order that first week. I was actually quite proud of myself for having unpacked half of the boxes by the time my husband got home a week later. We were excited for him to come home, and honestly, I just needed some alone time after that very busy, stressful week.

The first thing my husband said after walking in the door was, "Is this all you got done??!" It took everything I had within me not to knock him out at that point! I was furious! Did he remember that I had two small children and a hyper dog to take care of too? Did he honestly think I sat around the whole time with my feet propped up eating bon-bons? How dare him!!

I became even more stressed out because of his less-than-desirable attitude and the fact that things were still a mess and difficult to find. I am the type of person who needs things organized and kept in its place to function efficiently, so now that daddy was home it was his turn to take a little daddy time with the kids so I could finish unpacking. It was truly a great day worth celebrating when the last empty box left the house. Now I could concentrate more on just enjoying time with my kids again.

Shortly after the chaos of unpacking our belongings, Jake came home from work one day and discussed the idea of getting a computer. It sounded like a very good idea; he was going to be taking some classes. He said,

"This way I can be at home more and would not have to go to the library so much." He also suggested that a computer would be good to have so I could keep in better touch with my out-of-town friends. That being said, it made perfect sense.

Right after we made our new purchase, he began to spend all hours of the night as well as every evening on our computer and less and less time with me and the kids. It was like his escape from reality. It was very frustrating because I wanted to go out and spend time together as a family after being at home all day but instead, we ended up spending more and more time alone.

He was also noticeably becoming more irritable. At first, I just chalked it up to the stress of having a young family, the recent move, his new job duties and the fact he would soon be going back to school. A quiet tension began to build between us. I think the only thing that saved our relationship at that point was that he often traveled for business that first year we were there. It has been said that, "absence makes the heart grow fonder," and that was what I was really hoping for in this situation.

Things seemed to be getting better…for a while. Unfortunately, things went back to the way they were. I think part of the problem was that I was happiest when spending quality time with people, and he was happiest being alone and independent. I really wanted my little family to be close-knit because I did not have that as a child. It seemed as if my husband was fighting for his "freedom" away from us instead of trying to be a close family with us. His family was not close either, but it had the opposite effect on him and made him even more independent. As you can imagine, there was a definite tug-of-war going on.

Not long after we purchased our computer, I noticed that whenever I walked into the room, he would quickly click off the screen. Whenever I asked what he was doing, he would get defensive, but I think that deep down I realized what was really happening. Late one night, I walked in while his back was turned and he did not realize it. I saw that he was viewing pornography. Although I had a gut feeling that he had been involved with that, it still hit me hard to see actual proof of it. I was shocked, disgusted, very angry, hurt and betrayed! It was like a huge slap in the face! At that moment, I put the pieces together and realized this was why he was spending less and less time with us, and frankly, it had been like that from the time the kids were born. It was as if the pornography had been taking him away from us piece by piece. We were "competing" with something "better" that we could not possibly compete with and win.

I was such a mess for the next few days. I felt so fat and unattractive to him. I still could not believe my husband was involved with something so terrible and destructive. At that moment, I began to lose hope that our marriage was going to last forever. Honestly, at that point, I do not think I even cared whether or not it did. He later apologized and truly acted remorseful, saying he would not look at it again. But as much as I wanted to believe him, there was a significant drop in trust from that point on.

I remember very specifically, like it was yesterday, the day the Holy Spirit spoke to me during this dark time. I was driving home with the boys and right before we got home, the Holy Spirit's presence filled the entire car so strongly and clearly it almost felt as if a strong wind or force was in the car. At that moment He said, "Everything is going to be okay; I will be with you." From that moment on I have never been the same, and I know that the Lord sanctified me on that day! Later on, when I fully realized what had happened, I was filled with excitement and thought, "Oh yeah, I have reached the PINNACLE!!" I could sense the Lord chuckle at that naïve thought of mine as He said, "Oh no, my child, you still have a lot to learn yet." I must say He was very right about that!

So much in my life changed on that day! Some of the changes were immediate. For instance, I went from having a hunger for the things the world had to offer to having no desire for most of those things anymore. I did not realize before that time how much worldly things affected my attitudes and outlook on life (for the worst) until I no longer had a desire for them. I also went from a cup half-empty kind of person to a cup half-full kind of person. I had a deeper sense of peace and security at all times to a degree I had not had before that time. I also began to have a more consistent, deeper love and hunger for God than I had ever had before. From that point on, God spoke to me often and very clearly and intently in ways He never had before, for the first time in my life. (Although some changes were immediate, sanctification is also a life-long process that continues to this day). I knew by this powerful experience that God was preparing me for a battle ahead.

That same day, right after I got home, my husband confessed his addiction problem to me. It was at that moment I felt like the last bit of breath I had was kicked out of me. I felt so completely betrayed and shallow inside.

As devastating as that news was to hear, I was comforted by God's presence immediately. I realized at that moment that God was all I truly had. Not that I had grown far away from the Lord, but before this point God did not get as much of my time as He rightfully deserved. It was one of those very busy seasons in life with two small children to care for, and I was just trying to get through each day. I was doing well to squeeze in a very short devotional and a little thoughtful prayer time. Usually I was so dead tired at bedtime I would collapse into bed. I never had the luxury of having both kids down for a nap (so I could nap); my toddler decided the day I brought his baby brother home that he was no longer going to take another nap. He did not want to miss out on any excitement! Therefore, I had no quiet time until they were in bed at night.

Initially, I was so emotionally distraught at the breaking of this news that I cried often, because I felt like I had lost the husband that I loved very much. The Lord's strength was the only thing holding my pieces together at that moment so I did not literally fall apart. It was almost like a death, or at least the death of the relationship I thought we had. I really missed how things used to be before I found out about the pornography. I felt so ashamed that I had ever put Jake on a pedestal during the first few years of our marriage.

I tried hard to hold it together during the day because I did not want my boys to see me so sad. I also put on a "happy face" at church, feeling sick to my stomach each time I responded "fine" to the question, "How are you?" I knew I really was not fine at all on the inside. Most people do not have the time nor do they want to hear about your problems; they would rather hear that everything is great. My spirit felt like it had been crushed for a second time, the first time being when I was a child (although with God's help, I overcame that).

I was so ashamed of the pornography and it felt as if everybody knew our "dirty little family secret." It felt almost as if I had done something wrong and shameful too. I never knew that pornography could cause such a fierce spiritual battle, but there was definitely a battle being fought in our home. It seemed that the closer I drew to God and the more I was in His Word, the farther away my husband got. I prayed that the Holy Spirit's conviction would draw him away from the desires of pornography, and that our marriage would be healed.

For years, I have had the ability to sense evil presences or when something or someone is not right. This gift has protected me from several potentially dangerous situations throughout my adult life. Shortly after moving into that house, I began to sense a strong evil presence in our bedroom. I became terrified of being in that room alone, especially in the dark. I asked a friend from church to come over so we could pray over and anoint each doorway in the entire house. That very night, the presence was totally gone from the bedroom and for the first time in several nights, I peacefully went right to sleep. That event strengthened my faith to a new degree. As fierce as the battle was, I felt that good was finally beginning to win in that situation.

At this time I started focusing on and pouring over the Psalms, Isaiah and Job looking for hope and encouragement. I started praying small prayers constantly throughout the day about my situation just to be able to make it through each day. While I was in the shower, I would literally look up towards heaven and petition God to help me get through this and somehow save our marriage. I asked for mercy, grace and forgiveness for the ways I had behaved through this situation. I tried to be a good wife but knew that I had also fallen short, especially while having to endure all I was going through in this very difficult marriage.

One day as I was stumbling out of the shower with my eyes full of tears, I again looked up to heaven as I was praying and crying out loud to God for the strength to get through this, and I saw a vision of Jesus' face. It was full of sadness, and He had tears coming down His cheek. I kept blinking trying to clear my eyes, but it was still there. This vision really spoke to me because I could literally see and feel that Jesus was hurting right along with me as I was going through this and He truly cared about my hurt. That vision really encouraged me and gave me strength to face each new day of this nightmare I was living in.

I thought back to the words the Holy Spirit had spoken to me in the car, "Everything is going to be okay; I will be with you." Surely this meant the Lord was going to work a complete miracle in my marriage, heal all the brokenness and we would live happily ever after. It may, however, be a difficult road getting there so I would need to have patience and wait on His timing, because He would work things out and be with me in the process.

We attempted marriage counseling twice out of desperation. I was still hanging on to the white picket fence dream every girl has of being married, "happily ever after." The counseling ended up going nowhere for various reasons. However, the one good thing that came out of it was that the counselor anointed us each with oil, Jake for divine healing from his addiction to pornography and me to be freed from all of the hurt, anger and bitterness that had built up in me over the past few months. I did not realize just how much had built up in me until that point.

On my way home from that counseling session, I literally felt all of the bitterness, hurt and anger totally dissipate! I felt completely relaxed, calm and peaceful, which I had not felt in many months. It felt as if the Lord wiped all of those negative emotions away and I was starting all over with a clean slate. A huge burden and weight had been lifted off my shoulders at that moment. I experienced personally what **Matthew 11:28** says, *"Come to me, all who are weary and burdened, and I will give you rest."* (NIV) It was so amazing!

Although an amazing emotional healing in my life had taken place at that moment, we still had to live together and face each other day after day. The situation did not improve, but my attitude and outlook did. I felt more and more strength as if the Lord was holding me up, giving me the ability to keep fighting through this. Most of all, I was much more relaxed as this huge burden, which I was never meant to carry, was lifted off of my shoulders.

I have always been a fighter and a very determined person. I do not give up easily but this situation had really taken its toll on me. I was going to give it 110% and was determined not to be another statistic if only for the sake of the kids. I was even going to work on improving myself physically. I lost thirty pounds, got my hair highlighted and took greater care of myself, especially in my appearance. I thought if I looked better, then maybe my husband would become more attracted to me and fall in love with me all over again. However, this did not end up working as I had anticipated.

We finally had mutually decided that we needed a short separation time. Jake went to a hotel and was only gone a few days when he called me profusely apologizing for everything that had happened. He said that he loved me and promised to do whatever it took to make our marriage work. He also said how lonely he was and that he felt terrible for letting things get as bad as they did. Jake was gone for a total of six weeks and I thought that surely now things would improve because we were now on the same page and both willing to put in the effort needed to make this marriage work.

I continued to hold onto the faith that God was going to miraculously heal our marriage. We were not the only ones in a struggling marital relationship and I had seen other marriages healed. I also knew that God hated divorce and surely He would not allow it to happen to me if I just had enough faith and worked hard enough to prevent it. However, I forgot the fact that everybody has a free will. Even though I was willing to put in 110% into this marriage did not mean my husband would be willing to do the same.

I realized through this that everything in this situation was totally out of my control. Too many times in life I felt that I had things under control to a certain extent. However, this time was different. I fought as hard as I could to help the marriage work and nothing was happening. I finally had to relinquish total control to God and accept that this was not something I could fix on my own. By handing over complete control to God, I had to envision myself standing at the edge of an invisible "cliff" with my back turned. Totally by faith, I was going to have to fearlessly fall into God's arms trusting that He would catch me. Only by totally surrendering this to God and taking my own hands out of it could I move forward in the right direction. Whatever happened from this point on, I would choose to accept it even if it was not the outcome I wanted.

> *"Now faith is being sure of what we hope for*
> *and certain of what we do not see."*
> **Hebrews 11:1 (NIV)**

CHAPTER 5

Lessons in Forgiveness

Up to this point, forgiveness did not come easily to me. Therefore, I asked the Lord to help me forgive Jake AND all of those involved so that I could move on. Because of his involvement with pornography and the emotional "affairs" he was having, there were all of these "unknown women" who I felt were taking my husband away from me and the boys. It is hard to explain to someone who has not experienced this, but to those who have, I know you can relate.

At first, I questioned God as to why I even had to forgive him! He certainly did not deserve it for all of the pain he had caused. Also, every time I forgave my husband for one thing, he would turn around and do something else that hurt just as much. For instance, every time we went out somewhere as a family, he outright flirted with our waitresses and smiled at, enthusiastically acknowledging every cute young female we passed by, as if he were always trying to pick up a date. Each and every time, it felt like a slap in the face, and I would get upset and hurt all over again. It was like a vicious cycle.

The Lord revealed to me that forgiveness was like an onion and that there were many layers I had to "peel off." Armed with this new insight, I painfully went back and started naming each hurtful event that I was still holding onto. I verbally gave them, one at a time, to the Lord, forgiving my husband for each one. It was a long, difficult process.

What made forgiving Jake a little more difficult than forgiving my mother for her abuse was the fact that I still really loved him. Although it was hard to live with him day in and day out, there was still a shred of hope in the back of my mind that this marriage would work out. I told myself that maybe these problems were just temporary bumps along the way. I knew that it would be possible to forgive him after having already forgiven my mother, but I knew it would take divine intervention to help me once again.

It was imperative that I come to a point where I **made up my mind** to forgive him, not because he deserved it, but because I wanted to be able to move on and be free from the hurt, anger and pain I felt. The reason it was such a hard thing to do so initially was because I felt that if I forgave him, I was releasing him, in other words, letting him get away with all he did to me. To be honest, I wanted him to hurt as badly as he had hurt me! However, the following verse came into my mind: **Matthew 6:14-15,** *"For if you forgive men when they sin against you, your heavenly Father will also forgive you. But if you do not forgive men their sins, your Father will not forgive your sins."* (NIV) Ouch! Because I had not lived a totally sinless life and I, too, needed undeserved forgiveness by God, then I HAD to be willing to forgive my husband for his sins against me regardless of whether or not he deserved it.

Tensions were very high our last year there. We barely spoke to one another. For all we went through, we actually did not fight very often. There was more of a silent tension between us than anything else. I started to fear him, although up to this point he had never hit me. However, he often glared at me with intense anger in his eyes and I began to fear that he might try to physically hurt me. Although I began to fear him, I did not feel it was time for me to leave yet.

My prayers began to change from, "please heal my marriage, Lord" to "show me what to do and where to go with this." I truly wanted to honor my marriage vows and the Lord in the choices I made. I also needed to be sure that the Lord was releasing me from this marriage before I decided to leave. I was determined to do the right thing for the boys and the last thing I wanted to do was take them away from their daddy. This made the final decision excruciating for me to make.

Soon after that, my husband was on the phone discussing with somebody about how beautiful a particular girl was in her recent photo shoot with him. (One of the new hobbies he acquired was taking pictures of young models for their modeling portfolios). When he went upstairs to finish this call, I pulled the jack out of the wall, disconnecting his call. He came flying down the stairs, demanding to know why I did that. I actually thought it was funny…until he grabbed me around the neck and squeezed.

My oldest son had been taking karate classes during that period of time. Fortunately, I had gone to each of his practices and learned a few self-defense moves along the way. God knew that I would need these skills even before I needed to use them. Even before I could think about what to do, I took the heel of my right hand and hit Jake right in the sternum as hard as I could and he immediately released me with both hands. He did not even have enough time to hurt me, but it was enough to scare me!

First thing in the morning, I went to look for a place to rent. Every door in my path was closing. I could not find a single rental anywhere; everything was either way out of my price range, they would not accept dogs (and my dog was coming with me), or it was in a bad part of town. Frankly, I was not sure what to do at that point; I had been a stay-at-home mom ever since the boys were born and had been out of the work force for several years. It was a small city and there were not many decent jobs available in the area I lived so I prayed for God to protect me until I was able to find a job and a place to live.

While Jake was preparing to move to Georgia, I was contemplating on the possibility of moving back to where my family lived. I prayed a lot about where to go and what to do from there. Should I remain here with friends until I found a place or move back to my hometown?? Or, should I move on to Georgia, which was the last thing I wanted to do?!!

The Lord spoke to me very clearly and specifically said to "wait." That was quite unexpected, and also the last thing I wanted to do; however, I trusted that God knew what He was doing, so I did just that. One of the Lord's promises I claimed and depended on to keep me going at that time was **Isaiah 41:9-10**, *"I have chosen you and have not rejected you. So do not fear, for I am with you; do not be dismayed, for I am your God. I will strengthen* *you and help you; I will uphold you with my righteous right hand."* (NIV) He had not only verbally told me this, but showed me this truth daily throughout this particular time in my life.

Something very interesting happened right after the Lord told me to wait. We had to move into a new rental property about three months before we moved because our rental house was being torn down. Although I liked our neighborhood, it was a difficult place to live as a Christian because there were several people around us of a different religion who were quite antagonistic towards Christians. Although I thought the chances seemed slim to none, I prayed that when we moved to this new rental house that God would send me a Christian neighbor, specifically one in my church (a small denomination), who was a stay-at-home mom and had boys that my boys could play with. I knew that this could only happen by God's doing. At that time I really needed a good Christian neighbor who shared my beliefs, and with whom my boys and I could spend time.

Guess what?! After we moved in, I quickly discovered that two doors down there lived a family who was the same church denomination as I was, and she was a stay-at-home mom with two boys a little younger than mine! That was a huge answer to a very specific prayer! Imagine how my heart skipped a beat when I invited her and the boys to church only to find out that her grandfather had been a minister in this specific (small) denomination! They had just moved into the area and were looking for a church to attend, so we both had specific prayers answered that day!

Shortly after we met them, Joshua said he had awakened in the middle of the night and looked out his bedroom window located in the front of the house facing the driveway. He said he saw an angel standing out in the driveway, glowing brightly. I thought maybe he was just recounting a dream to me, but he was very insistent it was real. I prayed often that the Lord would send His angels to watch over our house and keep us safe from harm. It sent chills up my spine. How did Joshua know I had often prayed for that???

A few weeks later, the moving truck came and our belongings were packed up. It looked like we were headed to Georgia. At that time, I did not know why the Lord wanted me to move with my husband, knowing that my marriage was not going to last much longer anyway. However, I was going to step out in faith trusting that God knew what He was doing and that He would show me the reason soon…

> *"But they that wait upon the LORD shall renew their strength;*
> *They shall mount up with wings as eagles;*
> *They shall run and not be weary;*
> *They shall walk, and not faint."*
> **Isaiah 40:31 (KJV)**

CHAPTER 6

Georgia-Bound!

It was only by the grace of God and His plan for my life that the boys and I ended up in Georgia. The week we were officially supposed to leave, my husband told me that he was going to have the movers leave our belongings behind.

Initially, part of me was very disappointed because I thought that maybe the boys and I would be stuck here after all without a house or apartment. I was already geared up and excited to go to Georgia. Then I remembered that the Lord had told me to wait and not do anything; I had to remind myself that God would get us there one way or the other, if that is where He wanted us. As **Revelation 3:7** states, *"…What he opens no one can shut, and what he shuts no one can open."* (NIV)

Once we reached our destination, the first order of business was finding a house to rent. When we were looking at available rental houses, the last one stood out to me for several reasons. For one thing, I noticed a home security-looking sign on our way out of the driveway that read, "Protected by the blood of Jesus." WOO HOO!! What a blessing that would be…brothers and sisters in Christ living right next door! Now that I would be over seven hundred miles from home, this would be the next best thing to having family nearby. I could not wait to meet them! I felt completely at peace about taking that rental house and because my husband said the decision was mine as to which house we rented, I decided that was where I wanted to live.

Shortly after moving into the house, I met my neighbor's husband. He was a pastor of a Spanish-speaking church! He was quite fluent in English and very friendly. They always had family in and out, and soon I also met some of his extended family. A few nights later, I noticed a woman standing in the garage who appeared to be shy. My neighbor Ramon motioned me over and introduced her as his wife. I could tell immediately that she was not nearly as fluent or confident in her English-speaking abilities as her husband, so I began to speak to her in Spanish. Right away, she got a big smile on her face and was much more at ease knowing that I could speak her language. I was excited that I could finally put my Spanish-speaking ability to practical use again! I had not used it much since graduating from college so I had begun to lose a lot of my Spanish-speaking skills. Between the Spanish I remembered and the limited amount of English she could speak and understand, we communicated quite well.

I did not know this at the time, but I found out later that Ramon had told his wife right after we moved in that the Lord had told him that I was facing a very difficult time and that she needed to become friends with me. She kept saying, "No, that is crazy. She is always happy and smiles; there is nothing wrong." On the outside, we were quite good at hiding the fact that our marriage was on its last leg. However, Ramon was still very insistent in this, saying that the Lord had told him this specifically, so he continued to encourage our friendship. They started to invite me and the boys over for incredible home-cooked Mexican meals that would make any Mexican restaurant blush! During this time, I never let on that things were bad at home because their home was a place where the boys and I could just relax and have fun.

Even before we moved here, the Lord had already orchestrated everything to fall into place. This rental house had been available for quite some time and was just waiting for us…right next door to strong Christian neighbors…who spoke another language that I had studied for so many years and was able to speak and understand enough to communicate. Not only that, but the Lord planned our friendship early on by revealing to

Ramon that there was something wrong and I would need a special friend, which prompted him to befriend us immediately. It would only be a few months later that my husband moved out for good.

The few months prior to his moving out were filled with seeking direction on when and how the inevitable should happen. I knew the marriage was over already; I only prayed for the right words and the courage to tell my husband. One night, I came right out and told Jake I could not do this anymore. He had to make a choice between me or the model shoots and pornography; I was done sharing him. I had tried so hard to hang in there for six years while going through this daily nightmare, but I just could not do it anymore. Again, he was adamant he did nothing inappropriate; therefore, he had nothing to give up.

I still clearly remember the night before I gave Jake this ultimatum. I had a long conversation with God that my mind had been made up to leave this marriage. Right before this decision, the Lord made it clear to me that I needed to step out in faith and make the decision myself, not wait for Him to tell me exactly what to do and how to do it. I had to trust God enough to believe that He already knew the situation perfectly and would be with me and the boys through it all.

I was then again reminded of the Holy Spirit's words to me a few years prior to that: "Everything is going to be okay; I will be with you." After making that final decision, I was completely filled with peace and strength that I had not experienced about the whole situation in quite some time. To me, this was confirmation that I was being released from this unhealthy relationship. It was as if a huge burden had been lifted off my shoulders. **Matthew 11:28-30** came to me soon after, *"Come to me, all you who are weary and burdened, and I will give you rest. Take my yoke upon you and learn from me, for I am gentle and humble in heart, and you will find rest for your souls. For my yoke is easy and my burden is light."* (NIV)

Jake and I were very civil to each other after that conversation because I was more than ready for him to leave and he was ready for his "freedom." We agreed that for the kid's sake, he would wait until after Christmas, which was almost three months away.

However, that time frame changed when I accidentally backed into the front bumper of his car with my car. Unfortunately, he heard the commotion and came running outside, furious. There was a very large dent on the front right side of his car. When I got home later, he was not there.

When he did come home, he was still very upset and said that this was it. He decided to move out in the morning instead. Because I already knew this marriage would be over soon, I began preparing as soon as we had moved to Georgia by opening up my own checking account and putting away a little extra money I had earned on the side. I also began a food pantry in the attic. Part of me still panicked though because I had not even started to look for a job yet nor did I have very much money saved up. However, the other part of me was VERY relieved that this nightmare would finally be over!

He started to pack right after I left to take the boys to school. He said he wanted to be gone before they got home. My heart ached terribly for those boys who would be coming home to a house where their daddy no longer lived with no explanation or good-bye from him. After school, I sat them down on the couch to explain to them that daddy was not going to be living with us anymore, but they would still be able to see him sometimes. My heart completely ached for them as I broke this news while I tried (unsuccessfully) to hold back the tears.

Initially, Joshua handled it well, but my youngest son cried immediately. Little David was "daddy's boy," and it crushed my heart to have to break this news to him, totally unexpected. Afterwards, he sometimes had outbursts where he would cry or get very angry and frustrated for no apparent reason. Because he was so young, he did not know what to do with all of these overwhelming feelings. My heart broke for these very precious boys who were going through so much hurt and confusion.

I spoke with the boy's teachers and let them know what had happened at home, in case they should notice any behavioral changes in the boys. I did all I could to try and ease the transition for the boys to this new life. I also decided to stay in the rental house for another year in order to create some sense of security for them. I did the best I could to keep their daily routines the same in every area so that they would have some continuity in their lives.

That rental house was quite expensive each month and I had no idea how I was going to possibly find a job that paid well enough to cover the rent. Surprisingly, Jake agreed to pay the rent until we went to court and the child support started. This was definitely God's provision! When I did find a job, it was still a stretch on what little I made, but with God's help I made EVERY payment EVERY month and we never went without our basic needs being met. Through all of this, as difficult as it was, I faithfully tithed 10% on everything I made, including the child support. Only God could have filled in the cracks financially when my meager income could not.

That was the first time in my life I had to totally depend on God alone for all of my material needs to be met. Previously, I had either lived at home, on a college campus where my tuition, room and board were paid for, or with my husband. I worked full-time early in my marriage as did Jake, but I was never the sole breadwinner before this point in my life. I prayed daily for every single need to be met and had faith that God would provide my every need and would not leave us alone to fend for ourselves. **Matthew 6:25-26** says, *"Therefore I tell you, do not worry about your life, what you will eat or drink; or about your body, what you will wear. Is not life more important than food, and the body more important than clothes? Look at the birds of the air; they do not sow or reap or store away in barns, and yet your heavenly Father feeds them. Are you not much more valuable than they?"* (NIV)

I saw God provide even the smallest things. One time I was out of allergy medicine and did not even have the extra $10 needed to go get another box. My allergies had really flared up one day, and I was developing a pounding headache. Sometimes these headaches became migraines. I remember thinking, "I do not even have the money right now to get a stinking box of allergy medicine!" I felt physically terrible and emotionally discouraged. As I went to unload the laundry from the dryer a few minutes later, something fell out of the dryer onto the floor. It was a single blister pack with an allergy tablet in it. It was the funniest thing ever! The God of the universe, who determined the number of stars in the sky and calls them each by name **(Psalm 147:4)** cared enough about my allergies to send me an allergy tablet when I needed it most! Amazing!

Another time, my refrigerator was almost bare. I had to make what little was in there stretch as long as I could because I would not be getting paid until the end of the week. Realistically, I only had enough for one more day. I prayed, "Lord, I only have enough food for one more day. Help us make it to payday." For the next three days, every time I opened the refrigerator there was just enough for "one more day." During that week, my faith grew as He "multiplied" this food to make it enough to meet our daily needs. However, there were still times where I wondered when He was going to come through and how, especially when He provided at the very last hour. Because God gave me a specific promise out of His Word at that time which reads, *"You still the hunger of those you cherish; their sons have plenty,"* **Psalm 17:14b** (NIV) I knew that I would never have to worry about having enough food.

That was the first time, but not the last time, food was provided unexpectedly for us. We never had to go without a single meal, even during times of unemployment. I never asked the government to meet that need, but only depended on God to be faithful to His promise. There was only one time, and that was before I got my first job, when I had to go to a church food pantry. It was a very humbling experience and made me grateful that there was a church out there willing to fill that need for somebody they had never even met. What an important ministry that is to someone coming in off the street who maybe does not even know the Lord yet!

One time in between jobs, a lady in my church choir had shared that she had received a ticket for failing to yield at a stop sign and she did not know how she was going to pay it. She also said it was a good reminder to her about how she sometimes "fails to yield" to God and that there are consequences to that decision. Later that week, the Lord had laid it on someone's heart to pay the ticket for her. She then decided that because the Lord had blessed her, even though she deserved the consequence, she would "pay it forward" by unexpectedly stopping by my house one afternoon with a trunk full of groceries for us!

Financially, it was literally impossible for me to pay for all of our basic living expenses, considering how much income was coming in versus how much money was going out. I can say, however, that I faithfully kept tithing, even though Satan tempted me several times to quit tithing, and God faithfully provided every single need for us. I will be honest though by saying that there were times it was very difficult to tithe because of my low income, knowing how much I could really use that money. It was a gradual growth process that got easier each year. Three years later, I was finally at the point where I gave my tithe so joyfully out of every single paycheck that it was no longer even a temptation to hold back anything, regardless of how little or how much I had in the bank.

One of the times in particular when it was most difficult to tithe was right before my first Christmas as a single parent. I certainly did not have any extra money for Christmas gifts for the kids that year. I knew in my heart what Christmas was really about and there has always been a big emphasis on the true meaning of Christmas in my house (which did not include Santa); yet, to small children, a big part of Christmas is having presents too. I felt so inadequate and humbled at that time knowing that even though I was working full-time, I did not even have enough to buy them anything for Christmas. It really bothered me knowing that with all the boys had been through in the previous few months, I could not even provide them with a decent Christmas. I decided to pray that God would help me provide a nice Christmas for them.

I was very honest with the Lord about my hurt, disappointment and fears, and prayed that "I know this is not what Christmas is all about. It is really about Jesus' birth. Even if you never choose to do another thing for us, the gift of your Son is enough; however, if you could just help me make it a special Christmas for the boys, I would be so grateful." A few weeks before Christmas, a couple in my church handed me a card with $500 cash in it, not even knowing what I was facing that year.

Not only did the Lord hear my prayer and respond, He went way above and beyond what I had even imagined He would do! "Thank you" was not nearly enough to begin to express my gratitude and appreciation to God or this couple for what they did in our lives that year for Christmas. They not only provided gifts but an increase in my faith as well. Eight years later, I still tell the boys these stories to remind them how God has provided for us so faithfully through the years.

My second Christmas as a single parent, we received a grocery card to purchase food for a nice Christmas dinner, some gift cards and even cash for Christmas gifts. Though I had a little more money to work with that year, these things really helped us. Again, not a necessity, but God continued to shower us with His blessings and love when it was important to us.

The third Christmas, the boys had been "adopted" by their school's Angel Tree. I do not know who put their names on that list, but, again, the Lord provided so generously and unexpectedly through this huge blessing. We received a large laundry basket full of food (I also needed a laundry basket) as well as another big box of food to make another wonderful Christmas meal. The boys received clothing, shoes and more toys than they even really needed. It was very humbling, and even a little embarrassing at first because I was raised to be self-sufficient and never ask anybody for help nor accept help from anybody for anything. Because I had this ingrained in my mind, receiving help was, at first, hard to accept graciously. I think the Lord was trying to produce this type of humility in my life by not being too proud to accept help from others when I really needed it. I needed to learn to accept this type of blessing from Him. More than once I received so much blessing at one time that I was overwhelmed. I finally learned after several times to accept these blessings and not feel embarrassed.

Another time a friend at church gave me and the boys a card with some cash in it and an enclosed note that read, "I challenge you to tithe **20%** of this cash and watch what will happen. God rewards those who are faithful." Being a person who enjoys a challenge, I did just that. It was certainly not easy at that point though, as I had just started my single mom years and God was still growing my faith in this area of tithing when not having much income to work with. This friend never mentioned another word about that challenge; he left it between me and God. It was another step of faith in the right direction, and I never once regretted taking him up on his challenge.

One of the first things my husband said to me when I first told him that I was done with our marriage was, "You will never make it!!" I said to myself, "Watch me." Like I said, I enjoy a challenge. I would not trade the last several years as a single parent for anything. Although it has been very tough financially, I have made it. I have also been blessed through some great jobs with some amazing people I would never have met otherwise. I have also had opportunities to touch the lives of people I have worked with.

My husband was dead wrong because I *have* made it, not only because of my determination and hard work, but because of the prayer support and blessings of friends and family, and even more so because of God's help!

Looking back on all of these ways that God had so graciously provided for us, I have learned a lot about His love. It is far more encompassing than I ever imagined.

I am very grateful that before I became a single parent, He changed me into a person who depended more on Him and less on things to be happy. It sure has made this stage in my life much easier and better! He continued to tweak this ability in my life over the next few years so that today I can honestly say that the following verses are true in my life:

> *"...for I have learned to be content whatever the circumstances. I know what it is to be in need, and I know what it is to have plenty. I have learned the secret of being content in any and every situation, whether well fed or hungry, whether living in plenty or in want. I can do everything through Christ Who gives me strength."*
> **Philippians 4:12-13 (NIV)**

CHAPTER 7

Starting Over With a Promise in Job 8

While I was making the excruciating, life-changing decision to leave my marriage, I came across a particular scripture that jumped out at me like never before. It was **Job 8:5-7, 18-22** and I firmly believe that the Lord was giving me a promise through this passage, which reads,

> *"But if you will look to God and plead with the Almighty, if you are pure and upright, even now He will rouse himself on your behalf and restore you to your rightful place. Your beginnings will seem humble, so prosperous will your future be... But when it is torn from its spot, that place disowns it and says, 'I never saw you.' Surely God does not reject a blameless man or strengthen the hands of evildoers. He will yet fill your mouth with laughter and your lips with shouts of joy. Your enemies will be clothed in shame, and the tents of the wicked will be no more."* (**NIV**)

I can only reiterate how these verses spoke to me at that very moment I read them and how much they encouraged me as I was about to enter this new phase of my life. The Lord personally spoke to me in my situation through **verses 5 to 7** by reminding me that if I continued to live pure and upright, keeping God my primary focus, He would move on my behalf and restore me emotionally and physically. Although my "new" life (as a single parent) would be difficult in the beginning (financially, emotionally and materially), my future would flourish in all areas and all of my needs would be met.

In **verses 18 to 22**, He spoke to me by showing me that even though I was being "torn from my spot" (torn from my marriage and all I had known for the past twelve years) this part of my life would wither away and better, stronger "plants" would grow from this soil. Surely God would not reject me (NOT for living perfectly, but righteously and seeking Him with my whole heart), nor would my husband gain the upper hand over me. The Lord would again fill my mouth with laughter (which had been scarce for the last two years of my marriage) and I would be so filled with joy again that my lips would shout it out (and they already have)!

From the time I made the final decision and for the following few weeks, I felt an overwhelming peace. I soon realized how much God had prepared me ahead of time for this moment in my life. I was a much stronger woman than I had ever realized, which had been a gradual change in me over the five years leading up to this point in my life. I had also experienced the Lord's amazing presence in ways I never had before this time, such as in the vision, literally feeling His presence so strongly it was overwhelming, and in the times He spoke so clearly to me that I could hear it audibly, like He was in the room with me. These experiences gave me a rock-solid foundation to strengthen me. Every detail fell into place, and that totally amazed me. I was over seven hundred miles away from home in a strange city, but the Lord provided me with an extended "family" (my church) and great Christian neighbors to encourage me.

About a month after Jake moved out, I went to a ladies' retreat through my church. When I was invited to go, I told them I could not afford the $90 charge because of my new situation and they told me not to worry about that because they would take care of the cost for me. I knew it was going to be a very special weekend because I knew that God had worked it out so I could go for a reason. That retreat was exactly what I needed at that particular time in my life. I do not remember the theme of that retreat, but I do remember in particular the first evening during prayer right after one of the speakers got done sharing her heart with us. Something amazing happened that I had never experienced before.

I came to the retreat feeling very vulnerable because I felt like I was alone in the world having just moved to Georgia and knowing very few people in the area yet, combined with the fact that my husband had just moved out too. During that prayer, I literally felt arms wrap around me from behind and squeeze me gently. I thought it was one of the ladies I went to the retreat with, so I immediately opened my eyes to see who it was and nobody was there. At that moment, I knew it was the Lord reaching down and giving me a hug as a gentle reminder that He was there for me. I felt very refreshed from that point on and had a wonderful, relaxing weekend with the other ladies in my church group. **Matthew 5:4** most beautifully expresses that experience I had, which says, *"You're blessed when you feel you've lost* what *is most dear to you. Only then can you be embraced by the* One *most dear to you."* (MSG)

Although those first few weeks of being a single mom was likened to being knocked down to the ground over and over in a boxing match, I CHOSE to get right back up, brush myself off and tell myself I could do this. When forced into a difficult situation, we can sometimes be astonished at how strong we are. I thought I could not possibly have handled something this devastating, but with the Lord's help I was able to get right back up and move forward by pressing ahead and not looking back into the past.

After the weekend retreat, I resumed looking for a job, which was top priority at this time. I also volunteered at my children's school so that I could see them a little during the day, and they would know how important they still were to me. I also met them for lunch once in a while, but explained to them that once I got a job, I would not be able to do this anymore. They were used to me always being at home, so I had to prepare them for the upcoming changes that would take place when I started working.

One time in particular I surprised David by meeting him for lunch and he gave me the impression that he was embarrassed that I had shown up. I walked through the hot lunch line with him and when we sat down, I asked him what was wrong. He appeared to be self-conscious and asked me, "Why is everyone looking at you when they come into the lunch room?"

I was almost certain why he behaved like that; the boys had told me their father had told them right before he moved out that, "Mommy is too fat, ugly and old for me. I deserve better than that." I think David believed that this was what everyone thought about his mommy, so he was embarrassed because the kids were looking at me.

Although I was a little hurt and felt self-conscious when he said that, I answered his question with a big smile. "Why, David, don't you know?? They think I am so beautiful they cannot keep their eyes off of me!" From that moment on, David no longer acted self-conscious when I came to eat lunch with him. He actually asked me to come eat lunch with him again once I started working, although I was not usually able to do that.

When their dad first moved out, the boys also went through a period where they got anxious whenever I left the room for too long because they were afraid I had left too. I constantly had to reassure them that I would always be there for them and I would never leave them somewhere alone. Also, if I picked the boys up even a little late from school or from an activity, they got really worried that something had happened to me. Over time they got adjusted and this was not an issue anymore.

While the boys were at school during the day, I pounded the pavement looking for work. I tried my best to come up with a decent resume to send out; however, it did not look very promising considering I had been a stay-at-home mom for the last several years and my job history was lacking, to say the least. However, I had taken a few classes when we lived up north and with my new skill I became talented enough that I was able to make a little money on the side until I could find full-time employment. It also looked good on my resume that I had my own little side business.

I had been out of the work force for enough time that I was a different person going back into the work force; my interests and abilities had changed since the last time I had worked. I did not even know what type of job I wanted, so I applied for any job that sounded interesting. It took three months to finally find a job, as a mailroom supervisor. I enjoyed leadership positions and had some supervisory experience. It also seemed like an interesting job to me although it paid very little and offered no benefits. It was the first job offer I got, so I took it. For the most part, I really enjoyed the work. However, it was very challenging learning a new job, going through a divorce, being the strong one for my boys and being so far away from my family and everyone familiar to me.

When I first started the job, I was told that the woman before me had retired. Although they really missed her, everyone was very happy with having me there and enjoyed having me as their supervisor…except one person. Ginger was close friends with the woman who had retired and never wanted her to leave in the first place. She made it known she did not want her friend to leave nor did she want anyone else in her position. Although I was uncomfortable with knowing that, I really enjoyed this job and nobody else seemed bothered by the fact that there was a "new kid" on the block. Therefore, I did not let it prevent me from doing my best work.

Besides training new employees, I was in charge of making sure everybody worked efficiently so that mailing deadlines were met. I made sure all supplies were ordered, stock was kept up out in the warehouse, and packaging specifications were met according to postal standards. I had to set up each work station so that when the employees came in, everything would be easily accessible to them and ready to be assembled for that week's mailings. Then I would have to demonstrate to them exactly how the client wanted each mailing done. When each set was done, I would have to bundle them up correctly according to the postal standards and put them in postal mailing bags to be sent out to the post office. Ultimately, it fell on me if anything was late getting out.

However, not one time while I was the supervisor did we miss a single deadline; we always met or exceeded the deadline for each job. I quickly had a rhythm down and gave the part-time employees tips on how to increase their speed and accuracy. I soon formed a very good working relationship with all of the part-timers as well as with the operations manager. However, Ginger was making things very difficult for me by always trying to find something I was not doing "right," that is, differently than her friend had done it before she retired. I needed to do things a certain way that was easier for me so I could be more efficient and get the job done on time. The end result was always the same; I just went about working the process a little differently. Although I did make mistakes on the job at first, I quickly learned from them.

After almost a year at that job, the operations manager, with whom I had become good friends, called me into the conference room one day after everybody else left. I could tell she had been crying and she suddenly blurted out, "I was told that you have to turn in your keys and not come back to work." Right after she said that, she started crying and hugged me saying that she felt horrible about having to do that, knowing my situation, but it was her job; she did not think it was the right decision on the owner's part. She kept apologizing and asked for my forgiveness for having to fire me. I was completely stunned at the news I had just received to the point that I could barely speak. All I could do was cry and hug her back saying of course I forgave her and that I did not hold it against her (it was not her decision to begin with).

I was devastated, for I had grown to really love that job and the ladies with whom I worked. I think it would have been easier for me had I seen it coming or been incapable of doing the job or repeatedly missed deadlines. I was given no reason for being fired; the owner merely said he wanted me gone by the end of the day. I found out later that Ginger had constantly complained to the owner about everything I did, hoping they would get rid of me thereby making it possible for her friend to come back to work.

The rest of that week was a blur as I had to start over from square one again. I walked around for the next few days feeling numb and shocked at what had just happened. After the initial shock of it, I was able to think clearly and felt grateful that at least I had some good skills to add to my resume this time. However, the fact that I had gotten fired in slightly less than a year would not be helpful in my job search.

I was so ashamed of the fact that I got fired that I could not even share it with my church family for the first few weeks. I was hoping to get another job quickly enough that I would not even have to tell anybody what had happened. Again, self-sufficiency began to rear its ugly head. At first, I rationalized it by telling myself that I already knew that God had it under control and would work out the situation for me. Therefore, I did not feel the need to tell anybody about my embarrassing situation. However, what I really needed at that time were my brothers and sisters in Christ encouraging me and praying for me.

In the second week after losing my job, the Lord spoke very clearly to me and said, "Let my people help you." Immediately after I heard those words, I shared with my church family what had happened. After I did that, I had a great sense of peace about the whole situation. It was actually a relief and an encouragement to me to hear them lift me up in prayer and remind me that the Lord had something bigger and better waiting for me. People also began to help me and the boys in very practical ways to get us through that difficult time. I might add that through this time of unemployment, I continued to tithe 10% faithfully on what little was coming in through child support and alimony, and God greatly blessed me for that. Although I still did not understand why I lost my job in this way, I had faith that God would provide for my needs until I found a new job.

Another source of great encouragement was a promise that God gave me in **Psalm 37:25-26** just a few days after losing that job. It reads, *"I was young and now I am old, yet I have never seen the righteous forsaken or their children begging bread. They are always generous and lend freely; their children will be blessed."* (NIV) These verses reminded me that He would not let us go without our basic needs being met, even though the situation seemed bleak. In spite of the difficulties that came along with being unemployed, we were blessed in more ways than I could count as we saw God provide one need after another. Many times He went way above and beyond what I could have even imagined. There were so many blessings that I would have missed out had I gone with my original plan to keep this embarrassing situation to myself.

That was not the last time I went through a period of unemployment. However, I learned many valuable lessons through the first experience which really prepared me for the next time. I also learned that God was always going to provide for us during those times, so I had nothing to fear.

After a few months of unsuccessful searching, I finally decided to go through a temp agency thinking it would be better to have a temporary job than no job at all. It could also possibly open up doors for me in a good company after they saw how dedicated I was and how hard I worked. After about a month, I was sent for an interview at a cellular phone company for a "temp to perm" position. The first interview went well, but because I had no technical or sales experience, I did not expect to be called back for a second interview. A few days later, I was called to come in for a second interview with the branch manager and division manager. It also went very well, but again, I was not expecting to get hired because of my lack of experience. The following week, I got a call from the branch manager accepting me for the job.

After I picked myself up off the floor, I became very excited to start my new job! I found that the sales side of my job came easily to me, but having to navigate all of the different phones and be able to show our customers how to use their new phones did not. I also found it very difficult to successfully port phone numbers over and set up the initial phone service. None of it made any sense to me; it was like I was a round peg trying to fit into a square hole. After a few weeks at the closest branch to my house, they decided to move me over to another branch twenty minutes away because someone quit and they needed another employee at that location.

At first I was very disappointed and even found myself complaining about the move because the branch I was at was very busy with much more potential for better commission. The branch I was being moved to was in a much less popular location and not very busy. However, I decided to stick it out and try to learn the job anyway. I regularly became stressed out and frustrated because I quickly realized that this job was not a good fit for me at all.

I worked alone with a twenty-year-old girl who was very good at the job. She was very patient and encouraging along the way as I fumbled through my new job duties. I did enjoy her company when we had down time in between customers and other duties. I began to share with her what the Lord had done in my life and how faithful He had been to me through the some recent difficult times. She started to ask me questions which gave me more opportunities to share how much I loved the Lord and how He had blessed me even though I had been through a lot recently.

She admitted to me that she had gone to church and had a relationship with God when she was younger, but had turned away from Him over the past few years and messed up a lot along the way. One day, she said that she had really been thinking about our conversations and she was convinced that God had sent me there just to show her how much He still loved her and to encourage her to come back to Him and the church, which she did as a result.

That news alone made every frustrating moment of that job worth it! Now I knew why I had been hired for that job, because I had a mission to accomplish. The following week, the manager called me to let me know that she did not think this job was a good fit for me and that she could not hire me on permanently. Part of me was very relieved because from the start I knew as well as she that this was true. I dreaded going into work every day knowing I would have another frustrating day. However, it was still difficult knowing that I would have to start over again looking for another job, besides the fact that I got this news on Valentine's Day, which is not the most encouraging day for a new divorcee to get bad news. But, at least my mission was accomplished.

I learned an important lesson through that experience. I have never complained since then about which job God places me in because I learned that God always has me exactly where He wants to use me. Now I see each opportunity as a blessing from Him! Even though it was a difficult experience at the time, I still had the faith to believe that once again He would restore me to my rightful place and that "better, stronger plants would grow" out of this trial too.

> *"Though the fig tree does not bud*
> *And there are no grapes on the vines,*
> *Though the Olive crop fails*
> *And the fields produce no food,*
> *Though there are no sheep in the pen*
> *And no cattle in the stalls,*
> *Yet I will rejoice in the LORD,*
> *I will be joyful in God my Savior."*
> **Habakkuk 3:17-18 (NIV)**

CHAPTER 8

Thrown Stones

Many of those who get divorced do not get married to the love of their lives thinking, "I will try this marriage thing out; if it does not work, I can just get divorced." Neither do some people who end up divorced choose it; sometimes the choice is made for them. For example, a spouse may come home one day and say, "I don't love you anymore; I have found somebody else." Another example would be a physically battered spouse who needs to get out of a dangerous or even life-threatening situation for their protection. Other times, women in particular may endure physical and/or verbal abuse to the point that they psychologically snap before having the courage to leave that destructive relationship.

It is true; God hates divorce. He says so in the Bible more than once. He knows how destructive it is to the family and society in general. He also knows the consequences that come with it and the fact that there are always innocent victims, the children, who can be damaged for years as a result. Those facts also make a decision to leave a marriage even more excruciating for some people to make.

I only know that in my situation I wanted to exhaust every other possible alternative first before deciding on divorce. I prayed constantly and fought with everything I had, and it still was not enough. I left no stone unturned because I never wanted to look back with any regrets and wonder, "What if I would have tried this first? Could it in any way possible have worked out differently?" For that reason, it makes things even more difficult when people point and judge me on the basis of my marital status.

I like what Jesus said in **John 8:7** when a woman was caught in adultery, and the people were quick to condemn and about to stone her, that, *"If any one of you is without sin, let HIM be the first to throw a stone at her."* (NIV) He could easily have said that they had every reason to stone her, according to the law. But instead, He looked upon her with mercy. Instead of condemnation, He showed compassion. I wonder how many people who have been through the pain of divorce would have felt less lonely and more encouraged had more people (especially Christians) had Jesus' attitude towards them. Instead of automatically judging them as sinners beyond the reach of grace, what if others, more importantly other Christians, reached out in love and mercy as Jesus did, instead?

If Jesus physically showed up in our churches today, how would He reach out to those broken through the pain of divorce? Would He avoid them? Keep His family (if He had one) away from them? Treat them as if they had a contagious disease? Or would He reach out to them and simply show them love?

I have had both positive and negative experiences both within the church walls and outside the church walls ("church" being the church in general, not one particular church). I have had some show me great love, acceptance and compassion, treating me no differently than if I were still married. But I have also had some treat me as if I had a contagious disease and have actually pulled their families away from me, as if they were afraid that I would negatively influence their kids because my family is "broken." (Which, by the way, is a term that I strongly dislike because when something is broken it means it is useless, needing repair to be useful again).

It has been interesting to watch different people's reactions when they find out I am divorced. During the six years following my divorce, it was difficult telling people that I am a single parent (divorced) when they first met me and asked about my "husband." There was a little twinge deep inside of me that was afraid that they too would react negatively and pull away, even though they may not have intended to do that. There were even a few times during the first five years after my divorce that it felt like I was branded with a scarlet letter.

I am very grateful, however, that Jesus is full of love, mercy and compassion for the broken! Jesus would really stand out among the majority who have placed themselves in the role of judge, jury and executioner before even knowing what landed a divorced person in that situation. I am also very grateful for the many brothers and sisters in Christ who, like Christ, have chosen to stand out and reach out in love and mercy to those who are going through or have been through a divorce. Jesus said, *"As I have loved you, so you must love one another. By this all men will know that you are my disciples (followers), IF you love one another."* **John 13:34b-35 (NIV)**

Throughout the first three years immediately after my divorce, I was amazed at how many "friends" I lost. I suppose they were not really true friends to begin with, but it still hurt at the time knowing that again I was being rejected (the first time by my husband). I think some people meant well and merely did not know what to say or how to act around me, so they pulled away and said nothing. As prevalent as divorce is in our society, I was very surprised at the lack of support I found when I first went through my divorce.

However, I still found great love and comfort in knowing that the Lord Jesus was right by my side the entire time…even throughout the sleepless nights, teary days, and hardest moments. He never let go of my hand, not even for a moment. The same is true for anybody who turns to Him, no matter the situation. He will be right there with you, whether you are alone after divorce, sitting alone in a jail cell, or have just lost someone dear to you.

Allow Him to come in to your life and situation and comfort you through your darkest moments. I promise you, He will *not* let you down! He will also never make you feel like a second-class citizen because of your past mistakes or when you find yourself in a very difficult, lonely situation. He will not pull away from you when you need Him most or make you feel as if you are wearing a scarlet letter. There is hope, encouragement, and true love waiting just for you if you let Him in to help you and trust in Him to get you through. **Isaiah 41:10** says, *"So do not fear, for I am with* *you; do not be dismayed, for I am your God. I will strengthen you and help you; I will uphold you with my righteous right hand."* (NIV)

Too many people turn to something else, anything else, but Him to help them cope during a hard situation. For some reason, many people find it easier to turn to alcohol, drugs, cigarettes, sex or any other number of things to help ease their pain. However, they do not realize that those things may help temporarily to numb the pain, but the pain will ALWAYS come back, guaranteed. The Lord, however, will always be your help and will never leave you feeling empty or hopeless, so that you have to turn to something else to "numb the pain away." I can honestly say through my experience that He can permanently remove the pain if you let Him!

Although I have lost a few friends along the way and even felt shunned by some people, God also brought some amazing new friends into my life to encourage and love me through the divorce process and afterwards. Some of the friends I made while living in different parts of the country have still remained good, dear friends to this day. They were with me when things were tough and continue to be dear friends through the very best part of my life now. To this day, these friends and I enjoy talking about the wonderful things God has done and continues to do in our lives. We lift each other up in prayer and continue to encourage each other to grow even stronger in Christ. Because of God's help and encouragement and the love, support, and help of good friends during those early, lonely days He once and for all, *"turned my wailing into dancing; removed my sackcloth and clothed me with joy."* (**Psalm 30:11**) (NIV) I am very thankful for how He brought me through it and remained faithful to me when some were not!

I have had many people tell me how much they have been inspired, encouraged and strengthened through my life. Even though I do not realize it at the time, the way I handle difficult situations as a single parent often encourages others as they watch how I handle it. They say, "If you can handle that situation with strength, joy and grace, then it encourages me to do that, too." I am very encouraged when others tell me this, but I give God the glory because I realize that it is His strength in me that enables me to be strong during those times. **Isaiah 40:29** says, *"He gives strength to the weary and increases the power of the weak."* (NIV)

Although I have faced some very rough financial times, difficulties raising two boys alone, and periods of feeling overwhelmed with all of my responsibilities, I have been able to overcome each and every challenge that has come my way and eventually rise above them. I refuse to let them overtake and destroy me, even in those times when I have felt discouraged because we are "half" a family and I longed to have a "complete" family again. I try hard to look for the positive in every situation and try to make the best out of the situation I am in whenever possible. That does not mean that enduring these things comes easily or that I don't shed some tears in the process, but only that these things do not keep me down for long.

I am thankful that the days where I feel overwhelmed (with finances and all of my responsibilities), lonely, and even melancholy, are very few and far between. Just like everybody else, I have to pray my way through those times. I realize I cannot get through a single day without God's strength to help me. He always brings me encouragement on those days in one way or another. It may be through a song on the radio that really speaks to me at that particular moment, a sermon at church, a particular passage in the Bible, through His own voice, through a brother or sister in Christ, or even through a stranger to show me that He is still there with me.

During one of these times in particular a few years ago, I was having a "lonely, sad moment." Usually I only felt this way once or twice a year, either around Valentine's Day or close to my birthday. However, most of the time I am perfectly happy and content with my single parent status. That year for some reason I was fine around Valentine's Day, but it reared its ugly head over the summer. After posting a status on Facebook during that difficult moment, one of my dear cousins sent me the following note of encouragement:

> *Your status last night made me hurt for you. I wish there were some magic words I could say to you to take away your pain. I know you "know" all the right stuff. But I also understand*

that knowing the right stuff doesn't always help your heart to stop hurting. All I can say is that you ARE loved! You are loved because of who you are and that's better than being loved because of how you look! I know it may not come in the form of love from a man, but I know you have plenty of people around you who love you because of who you are! Hold your head up high, smile and enjoy life one day at a time… with every little joy and blessing God gives. As hard as it is, try not to look at what you don't have but try to find all the beautiful and precious things you DO have. :D (I know you do this already anyway). I just wanted to let you know you ARE loved and that I prayed for you! Now smile and go on being the BEAUTIFUL PERSON YOU ARE! :D

Although I have these once-in-a-blue-moon moments when I feel lonely, discouraged or just plain overwhelmed, I am most grateful to God that I have not become permanently embittered through my divorce! That alone is amazing to me, and I consider it a blessing because I see so many people who have been in my shoes who are angry and bitter for years afterwards. They are still fueled by hate for that spouse and the difficulties that came as a result of their divorce. My attitude is, what's done is done, and I have chosen to forgive my ex-husband. Today we have a decent, and most importantly, civil relationship.

I chose very early on to become better and stronger through this. **The very same thing that causes some people to turn away from you may be just the thing that God allows to help shape you into the beautiful person you are meant to be.**

If you have been divorced, I challenge you to help and encourage somebody else going through it. Also, forgive your spouse for the pain they caused you and do not allow it to embitter you. If you have not been divorced, I challenge you to be there for somebody who is and just needs your acceptance, love, and encouragement. Treat them as Jesus would treat them, and not as if they had something wrong with them. Isn't that what we are called to do anyway???

"Each of us should please his neighbor for his good,
To build him up. For even Christ did not please
Himself but, as it is written: 'The insults of those
Who insult you have fallen on me.'
…Accept one another, then, just as Christ accepted you,
In order to bring praise to God."
Romans 15:2-3, 7 (NIV)

CHAPTER 9

A New Home

I was blessed to be able to drive the boys to and from school every day, even after I started working. I always thought that the subdivision of houses surrounding the school was so beautiful as I drove down into a sea of beautifully lined up houses and trees each morning. It was no more special than any other neighborhood, but something about it was very peaceful and caught my eye. However, at that time, I was completely happy where I was already living. One day in particular I thought, "I wonder if these people realize how blessed they are to live in such a beautiful neighborhood. I hope they do not take it for granted." I was not even thinking that far ahead yet, but a few years down the road, God blessed me with a house in that very neighborhood!

When the time came to renew my second-year lease on the rental house, I decided that it was time to buy a home. I already knew I loved the part of town I was in and that the boys and I were going to stay in the local area anyway. Besides that, the rent was about ready to go up again, and it was getting harder on my small hourly wage to make the rent payments, and a mortgage would cost a lot less per month than renting.

I started praying very specifically about six months ahead of time for what I needed and even those things I wanted in a house. Besides staying within my budget, I needed to have a fenced in yard for the boys and the dog. Because my oldest son and I have a cigarette smoke allergy, I needed a house with previous non-smokers. I also needed a safe neighborhood in order to not have the added stress of worrying about our safety. Most of the houses within my price range were neither in the best neighborhoods nor the best school districts. If they were, the houses were so tiny that I could not have even fit what little furniture and few belongings we did have in them. I really wanted to leave the boys in the same school district so they would not have to change schools. I felt the need to keep as much consistency as possible for the boys.

There were also some things that I had prayed and hoped for, but they were not necessities. Ever since moving here, my Jacuzzi tub had become a special place to me every night for my prayer and devotion time. That was one thing I wanted to continue in my new home, too, so I prayed for one of those tubs.

I also prayed that the boys would each have their own bedrooms; I knew that in a few years they would be teenagers and need to have their own individual space. Not that I wanted anything big, but just a comfortable size for me and two growing boys. I also knew that most likely I would be living in that house for the rest of my life. For financial reasons, I prayed that the appliances would be included so I would not have to purchase new ones. Also, I preferred an attached garage (for safety reasons), and a decent-sized yard. Even more importantly, I asked for a quiet neighborhood with good neighbors, as I had already experienced living in a loud neighborhood with difficult neighbors when we lived in our last city of residence.

I found a realtor through the rental company from whom I was renting my house to help me find a house to purchase. I had a good two-year relationship with one of the owners of the rental company, and I knew I could trust whomever they recommended. I was very happy when he told me that his mother was a realtor, and he gave me her contact information.

Before she could even start looking for a house, we had to do all of the paperwork to be sure I qualified for a loan. I was honest and said I had not even been at my job for three years yet, which was the minimum qualification to get a loan. My previous job history had been sketchy; therefore my odds of qualifying did not look good from that standpoint. However, I had total faith and trusted that God would somehow make it possible when it was the right time for me to purchase a home. I had only been at my job for a year-and-a-half at that time. Because I really needed to be making smaller monthly payments than I was for the rental house, I felt an urgency to purchase a home at that particular time.

A small down-payment was, of course, required on the house. Because I had no savings at the time (as I had to start all over financially on my own), that would not be possible for me. My realtor told me that I may qualify for special assistance given to first-time home buyers who needed help getting into a home. I filled out the paperwork, went to a three-hour meeting and found out all about this program and my responsibilities in order to get this financial aid. As long as I stayed in the home for seven years, I would not have to repay the money back. However, if I left the house for any reason within the first seven years, I would have to pay it back.

I was still a few thousand dollars short to get into the house, so I decided to ask my dad if I could borrow the money. I had never asked him for any help since becoming a single parent, but in this situation I knew I had to try every resource possible to get into a home. It was a very hard thing for me to do because I really hate asking anybody, even family, for money. However, I knew that this few thousand dollars was standing in the way of me purchasing my own house. He graciously said he would be glad to help me in order for me to be able to have my own place to live and not to worry about paying him back. The Lord worked out a lot of details like this so I could have my own place to call home!

My realtor called about a week later and said she had three houses she wanted to show me. We went to look at the first two but were not able to look at the third one quite yet because the owners were not available to show it to us. I thought the first two were adequate but a little on the small side; I liked the second house better than the first. However, it was a zero lot line so really had no yard for the boys and our dog. The back yard was backed up to the woods and had no fence. However, the house itself was beautiful. I thought I would wait to see the third house before making a decision.

I knew that God would make it clear to me which house He had for me, and I did not have that feeling with the first two houses. I found out later that my ex-husband's girlfriend, who later became his wife, lived in the same neighborhood right across the street and down a few houses from the second house I toured. Once again, God protected me from a potentially bad decision because He already knew this fact and that it could have caused problems for all of us down the road.

As we went through the third house, it had everything I needed; it was also in a safe neighborhood, had a fenced in back yard and it was a little bigger than the rental house. I knew that my furniture would fit. The appliances were included too, except that the refrigerator was negotiable. My realtor said she would ask for that in the contract as well, so I would not have to buy one. The house was only three years old and still in excellent condition. It had a slightly bigger front yard and a much bigger back yard than the rental house.

The carpet in the den had two small places that had been torn up by the owner's dogs, but other than that, the flooring was in perfect condition. I really was not concerned about it because the spots were small and in a place that could easily have been hidden, but the owners offered to either replace all of the carpeting in the entire house or put down a hard wood floor in the entry way and den if I decided to buy the house. They were very motivated to sell because they had bought some land the year before and were in the process of building a bigger house for their growing family. This house had been on the market for just over a year. The only reason I could have even possibly purchased that house was because they had just lowered the price by $10,000, which put it right within the range of my budget!

As if that were not enough, it had everything that I needed and prayed for, which included a larger, deeper Jacuzzi tub than the one I had previously, a full attic, and about 220 square feet more than our rental house! It also came with several bonus upgrades, including ceramic tile flooring (instead of linoleum), plant ledges in the master bath and over the kitchen cabinets, a bay window in the kitchen, and all of the plantation blinds were already installed and included in the package…not to mention the hard wood floors they offered to put down for me.

After consulting with my realtor, I told her that this was the house I wanted. We then made the offer, which they immediately accepted. Obviously, we did not have to bargain on the price, for it had just been lowered significantly in order to sell, but we did ask for the refrigerator, which the owners had said previously they wanted to take with them. Because the house had been on the market for such a long time and so many people had looked at it without even making a decent offer, they were very motivated to sell. This really worked in my favor.

I know that the reason it was on the market for such a long time and did not sell was because God had my name on that house the whole time. The best part about it was that it was on the *very street* that I drove down every day to take the boys to school. The same beautiful neighborhood where I had previously wondered if the people living there realized how blessed they were for living in such a beautiful place. I knew one person who did realize how blessed she was for being able to call this neighborhood home! I never dreamed I could even afford a home in that neighborhood. It made me even more grateful for this very special gift that God picked out and hand wrapped just for me!

Many details fell into place. First of all, my job history should have financially disqualified me from getting a house in the first place. Only God could have worked out every little detail with such perfect precision that a single mom like me could have a nice little house to call her own. As a father lovingly provides for his child and a husband for his wife, the Lord had wonderfully provided a huge need in the most unlikely way possible… not because He is a genie who grants our every wish, but because He loves me, wants the best for me and He just enjoys blessing His people. As **Matthew 7:11** says, *"If you, then, though you are evil, know how to give good gifts to your children, how much more will your Father in heaven give good gifts to those who ask him!"* (NIV)

The house was also in a very ideal location and only five minutes away from my rental house. It was only ten minutes away from everything I needed but still far enough away from the noise and traffic on the main streets. It was about a mile-and-a-half from my job and a half mile from the church we were attending at the time. It was also around the corner from the boys' school. It sure saved on my gasoline bill by living so close to everything!

The Lord opened many doors that seemed impossible in order for me to have my own home. After everything else He had already provided for me, this was like the icing on the cake. Every day for the first few years I lived in this house, I could not help but cry tears of gratitude as I thanked God for this huge blessing. I was in such awe of the fact that He opened that many doors to make it possible for me to even become a homeowner.

From day one, I promised the Lord I would open my home up to anybody who needed it and would use it to minister to others in any way I could. This was His house anyway; He just gave me the privilege of living here and taking care of it. Thank you, YAHWEH YIREH…the God who provided! For God saw my future, my present, and my past and was willing and able to provide what I needed when I needed it!

CHAPTER 10

Hope Found Amidst a "Hopeless" Situation

After being in my new house for about a year-and-a-half, the economy took a big turn for the worse. The contracting and building industries were really beginning to suffer at the time, so the particular company I was working for was hit hard too. I worked at a wholesale business that sold doors, specialty glass, windows, trim, casing and molding to builders. Because many builders either had to slow down or quit building houses, we were also losing business quickly. This naturally led to a lot of layoffs where I worked. I survived the first three or four rounds of layoffs, but inevitably, my head was eventually place on the "chopping block" and they laid me off.

As Mr. Thomas called me into his office, I knew exactly what was going to happen even before I sat down. I could see that he was upset about having to break this news to me, as we had become friends. He knew how hard I worked every day, did my work completely and accurately without having to be told and I was always on time. Everybody there was close, like a family. It was hard watching parts of our family leave each time there was another round of layoffs.

As I sat down with Mr. Thomas, he told me that through no fault of my own, business was slowing to the point that he had no other choice but to lay me off. He said that they tried to hold onto me as long as possible, but could not keep my position open any longer. He went way above and beyond what he even had to do for my severance package because he knew that I was a single mom. I was very grateful to him and the Lord for looking out for my best interest in spite of the situation.

Although I could see it coming, it was still very hard to accept in the beginning. Working there was so enjoyable each day as their front desk greeter and receptionist. The job itself was not too interesting but the people I worked with were entertainment in and of themselves and some of the funniest people I have ever met! Being one of only two females working in the front office, you can imagine that we were targeted in jest many times. I also had to watch my back because there was a major prankster whose office was directly across from the front reception area. He tried to scare me one by putting a (fake) snake inside a box and putting it on my desk. I told this jolly prankster, "Sorry, man but if you wanted to scare me you should not have used a fake snake because I am not afraid of them." However, I am terrified of bugs so I am glad he did not try the prank using a fake giant bug. I have so many good memories of that place.

After I was laid off, I still dropped by occasionally to visit because it lifted my spirits. Compared to that working environment, my house was quiet and lonely during the days when the boys were at school. Typically, I am a very social person, so it was difficult to be alone all day (although I kept somewhat busy looking for a job), when I was accustomed to being with others.

Right before being laid off, I had decided that if I were ever laid off I would go back to school to learn a new trade. I had a bachelor's degree but felt that I had not accomplished much with that degree. I was not sure what type of work I wanted to do so I started praying that the Lord would open doors for me in a trade program or job that I would excel in and enjoy.

One day, I was reading a magazine to get some ideas for a new career field and/or schooling. I had no desire to go back to college full-time because being only average in intelligence and a slow learner, I had to devote an excessive amount of time and work in school and knew that I had to get another job soon too. With being a single mom, I knew that personally it would be too difficult to handle a job, full-time school and raising two boys alone. A three- to six- month training course would be perfect for me. I came across an ad for a six-month medical transcriptionist program and knew it would be a perfect job for me once I finished. I was always good at typing, grammar, editing, and have always had an eye for detail. I had also studied in the medical field the first two years of college so I was quite familiar with medical terminology. Another thing that made this decision easier to make was knowing that the six equal monthly payments would be affordable, and this program would be paid for in full by time the course was over. Again, God provided the means out of my very meager pay for me to make each school payment as it came up, so I had no school debt after getting my certification!

Two weeks after being laid off, I got a very surprising phone call from that company's operations manager. She said that there was a purchasing assistant job that really needed to be filled because the person in that position quit. She wanted to give me the first opportunity for that job before they advertised it outside the company. I immediately accepted the job and started the next day. The pay was the same amount I was making before I was laid off and the benefits were also the same. However, because it was such a short period of time between when I was laid off and re-started back to work, they maintained my insurance and paid days off as if I had not even left there at all! Although it was a higher position than I had previously, the pay would be a lateral move. At that point I did not care what I would be making; I was just thrilled to be asked to come back and work again!

I knew that this job too would most likely be temporary unless the housing market improved to the point where we could start gaining more business again. At least I had a job for now anyway, and I was so grateful for that! However, I knew it would also be very challenging this time around because I had already committed to the medical transcriptionist schooling, so I would have to juggle both working full-time and homework on evenings and weekends as well as taking care of my responsibilities with the boys. There were many times I was very overwhelmed and stressed out, but I knew that eventually this would pay off. Besides, it was only temporary. Medical transcription was the perfect fit for me and I knew I would really enjoy a job in that field should I be laid off again.

Shortly after finishing the transcriptionist schooling I was laid off again, this time for good. A lot of other people were also laid off in every department the same time I was; they would be working on a skeleton crew after that. This time, I knew what I wanted to do for a career. I applied for what seemed like hundreds of jobs that I heard about by word of mouth, read in the paper and saw online. I went to job fairs with resumes in hand and applied for several different types of jobs but heard back from very few employers between all of these avenues. I was primarily looking in the medical field but learned very quickly it was nearly impossible to get a job in medical transcription without at least a year of experience. I was hoping that I had not made a mistake by going back to school and working so hard to get certified in medical transcription. How could they expect anyone to get experience if they would not even hire you without any experience??!!

There were several months where I did not hear a single thing back from any potential employers, although I felt half of Georgia had my resume. I began visiting any company that was hiring and leaving my resume to no avail. It was very discouraging to wake up day after day, month after month trying so hard to find a job with absolutely no word back from anybody, especially after working so hard to get certified in a new trade.

There were days when all I could do was cry and pray. After several months of being unemployed, I began to feel useless because as the main breadwinner for my family, I inadvertently began to tie part of my value to having a job. When I began to do this, the Lord gently reminded me that my value was in Him alone and did not depend on my job status. Sometimes, a seemingly hopeless situation can cloud our vision and make us forget the truth.

By being in this situation, I was made brutally aware of what men (traditionally the main breadwinner in the family) went through when unemployed, unable to provide for their families. I also witnessed first-hand how much our society places value on a person who has a job. One of the first questions everybody asks when they first meet you is what you do for a living. This is one of several examples of how our society misplaces the value of a person.

The discouragement finally came to the point where I became downright irritable whenever somebody asked me if I had found another job yet. I knew they meant well, but it was getting more difficult to tell them that yet another week or month had gone by without even a job lead.

I made them fully aware of the fact that it would be obvious to everybody as soon as I got a job.

Because I now had more free time, I took the opportunity to volunteer in the church office once a week. It felt good to get out of the house and take a short break from spending all day tirelessly searching for a job. It also helped having adult conversation during the day, even if it was only one day a week. My friend, who worked in the church office, took me out to lunch on Fridays. It was such a refreshing break each week and it felt good knowing that I was contributing to society again.

I also started attending a Monday morning women's Bible study. I was so encouraged by the other ladies as they prayed for me every week. Not **only** did they pray for me to find a job soon, but they also prayed that it would be a job that I LOVED, that I would have favor in the eyes of my employer, and that I would be successful at this job. We believed in faith that God was going to do something much greater than give me just any job. The ladies also prayed for all of my needs to be met until then.

The beauty of that particular Bible study, besides the encouragement from the ladies, was that every week the lesson spoke directly to me in this particular situation. I cried tears not only from sadness because of this situation, but more importantly tears of gratitude to God for speaking to me through each lesson. I felt His presence so strongly during each lesson that I was empowered to face the rest of the week. There were still days that were very hard to get through, but I began to feel more inspired to continue in my job search each week until the ladies met again the next week.

After six months, this situation seemed hopeless to me. Busting my chops day in and day out with no hope of even an interview really began to discourage me in a huge way. Although I was very, very grateful for unemployment benefits, every time I went to the bank to deposit my check I could not help but hang my head in shame. I could not get out of that bank fast enough. I worked so hard at trying to find a job and had a college degree and now certification (which I also worked very hard for), for crying out loud! I should have had a job by now!!

However, God provided every single need the entire time I was without a job. I continued to make every house payment and pay every bill on what little I got for child support and alimony. At least it was temporary, I told myself. We would not have to struggle like this forever. It was obvious that the Lord held us in His hands throughout the entire eight-month period, even during the saddest moments. He showed me several times in many ways how much He cared for me and the boys.

For instance, He often laid it on people's hearts at church to do something for us by helping with our material needs throughout that eight-month period. A few people told me that the Lord had led them to give me a gift card to buy the boys some clothes or groceries. A friend of mine at church even took me out for a special lunch at her favorite tea room. I had only been to one tea room before so it was extra special to me. All of the little things really did make a big difference!

There was one difference this time that distinguished it from the other times I was going through a very difficult financial season. Although it took a few times of being in a similar situation, I was finally able to accept help graciously from those wanting to help me. It was much easier that time accepting help with a grateful heart. It touched me to see how good people felt when they were able to help us.

One day in particular I was having a really, really bad day. I woke up crying and I spent the entire morning praying out loud to God. I said, "If you would just show me HOPE that there's a job out there for me, I could handle this better. All I'm asking for is some HOPE right now! Something…anything!!" About 30 minutes after I finished praying, the doorbell rang. I was still in my robe and completely baffled as to who would possibly be at my door this time of day. My neighborhood was normally very quiet all day long and I was not expecting anybody to come over.

At first, I thought it was probably a sales person. I looked out the peephole and saw my friend Jane, also a single mom, with whom I used to go to church. She had not been by my house in over a year, so I was quite surprised to see her on my doorstep. I opened the door and she immediately said, "I don't have a lot of time because I am on lunch break from work and have to get back, but the Lord told me to stop by and give you this CD. I almost drove past your house because I am running late, but the Lord would not quit telling me to stop and give you this NOW." I thanked her and could not wait to listen to it.

Would you believe that every song on there, with the exception of one or two, was about hope?! Hope in the Lord, hope in the midst of our difficulties, and the hope we have for a good future because He is The Lord who watches over us and takes care of us. I was in such awe of God after listening to those songs that all I could do was thank Him over and over for showing me that there was hope in my situation. He spoke to me through that CD for the next few months until I would finally get a job. I claimed every word as God's promise to me because I knew it had obviously come directly from Him. I was encouraged every time I listened to it. It gave me the hope I was looking for when I really needed it!

As **Job 11:18** says, *"You will be secure, because there is hope; you will look about you and take your rest in safety."* (NIV) I find it incredibly encouraging that the Lord reaches down and gives each one of His children the hope they need. Not only this, but He gives hope at exactly the right moment in the way it is most needed. Through His willingness to give us hope during a very difficult time, we are able to feel secure and rest in His safety knowing that He will meet our every need. We may still have hard days in the midst of our difficulties, but He will walk us through them and give us the strength we need to make it. He will not only use what we have been through to strengthen our faith in Him, but He will also give us the opportunity to use this to help somebody else going through the same situation. **II Corinthians 1:3-4** says, *"Praise be to the God and Father of our Lord Jesus Christ, the Father of compassion and the God of all comfort, who comforts us in ALL our troubles, so that we can comfort those in any trouble with the comfort we ourselves have received from God."* (NIV)

After playing that CD every day for almost a week, I had a newfound energy to go out and hit the pavement even harder this time to find a job. During this week, I also began to pray for some career clothes because my closet was really lacking in dress clothing. At my previous job I wore jeans every day so I did not need dress clothing, except for church. If I was going to start a career soon in the professional world, I knew I had to look professional. Because I had not worked for so many months, I did not have any extra money to buy career clothing, so I decided to pray in faith that the Lord would provide once again. God knows our basic needs of food, shelter, and clothing so we have nothing to worry about when it comes to those needs because He will always provide.

Matthew 6:28-30, 33-34 states, *"And why do you worry about clothes? See how the lilies of the field grow. They do not labor or spin. Yet I tell you that not even Solomon in all his splendor was dressed like one of these. If that is how God clothes the grass of the field, which is here today and tomorrow is thrown into the fire, will He not much more clothe you, O you of little faith?"... "But seek first His kingdom and His righteousness, and all these things will be given to you as well. Therefore do not worry about tomorrow, for tomorrow will worry about itself. Each day has enough trouble of its own."* (NIV)

The following week, a lady from church called and invited me to her house to go through some of her clothes. She was doing some major closet-cleaning and had all sizes of dress clothes, shorts and pajamas to choose from. She said I could take whatever I liked and as much as I wanted. When I got to her house, she had five enormous piles of clothes to go through. About half of them were beautiful dresses, skirts, and blouses that were my size. I went home with more beautiful clothes that I could have ever purchased on my own! A lot of them looked like new and a few of them even still had the tags on them. They were of high quality too, so I knew that they would last for a very long time and not need to be replaced for several years. Once again God answered my prayers so specifically and went way above and beyond my wildest dreams!

This gave me a big boost of confidence and more incentive to continue job searching at an upcoming job fair, even though I received no responses back from the last job fair I attended. I now looked and felt professional and had regained much of the confidence I had lost during the previous seven months of unemployment. I was ready once again to conquer the world! (At least from a job-searching perspective).

Like the last job fair, I left resumes with several potential employers and even had a few quick interviews. My last stop was at the medical jobs section of the fair. I left resumes for three of the medical jobs that I was qualified for, one of which was for a medical transcriptionist job! I almost passed right by without leaving a resume with them because the job description said you had to have a minimum of one year experience in medical transcription, which I did not have. On top of that, almost an entire year had lapsed since I had received my certification in transcription, so my chances of even getting a call back were very slim. However, I still wanted to get my resume out there to as many hospitals as I could in case any job opened up in the medical field.

I did not hear anything back for two weeks, but then the call came that I was hoping for! The department manager from one of the hospitals represented at the job fair called asking if I would come in for an interview for the transcriptionist position in the cardiology lab. That was exciting because I was not expecting to hear back from that particular job, due to my lack of experience! However, I still firmly believed that miracles happen when God becomes involved in the process! Nothing else matters, even lack of experience, if the Lord wants you in that place for a reason. Knowing that I would get this job if it was where God wanted me, I was able to go in with a confident attitude that said I already had the job.

The interview was only about fifteen minutes long. The department manager just explained the job responsibilities and specifics of the job. She said that I had a very good resume and she had another interview later that day and would get back to me soon. Because it was such a brief interview, I certainly did not leave there feeling confident that I had that particular job. However, less than twenty minutes after I left the interview, I received a phone from one of my references. She said that this manager had already called her. Another one of my references advised me on the same day that she also received a call. At that point I felt I had a great chance of getting this job and I was already thanking the Lord!

The next morning, I got the phone call offering me the job and they wanted me to start orientation on Monday! Although it was only on a per-needed, part-time basis, I was still ecstatic because I knew that I could find another part-time job to make up more hours. The drawback was that it was a 35-minute drive each way in very heavy interstate traffic. However, at that point it did not matter because this was my first viable job offer that paid decently enough to make it worth the drive. I now had my foot in the door so it would be easier to find another part-time job within the hospital to make full-time hours. Whenever new job postings were listed, I looked to see if anything was available that I qualified for. There were very few part-time jobs I even qualified for that were listed and most of them were third shift or weekend positions, which were not conducive for a single parent; however, I kept patiently waiting. I knew that something would open up sooner or later because God knew that I needed another job.

About five months later the department doctor, a good Christian man, asked me if I was looking for another part-time job. I told him that I was indeed looking for more hours, so he asked me to fax my resume to his house and his wife would call me about a job opening at his practice. The next day, I faxed it to her and that night she called saying she wanted to meet with me. I started working at his practice the next Tuesday on my days off from the hospital. I was very excited to finally be working full-time hours again! His office was right across the parking lot so it was easy and convenient.

Before I started working at his practice, his office manager (who is also a Christian) sometimes stopped by the cardiology lab. I also had several opportunities to speak to her on the phone. She was always very sweet and I remember thinking that it would be really nice to get to know her. Now I would have the opportunity to work closely with her. It was a very small office with only three employees on Tuesdays and Thursdays, which were patient days. We hit it off from the beginning. She was the one responsible for training me and had the patience of a saint! She also had a knack for dealing patiently with people who were irate or just plain difficult to handle. I was hoping that some of her patience would rub off on me, because that was one quality I needed to have more of in my life! Although I have learned to become much more patient than I used to be (with God's help), there was still a lot of room for growth in that area!

Most of the time, I worked full-time hours between the two jobs. However, there were a few occasions where I was not needed in the cardiology lab so I had a day off. There were slow periods at the hospital where I would not have to go in for a few weeks at a time but fortunately that was not very often. Because I was part-time and had no paid time off (sick days, vacation or personal days) there was a noticeable difference in my pay checks when I was not there every day; I needed all the hours I could get in order to get my household running smoothly again and start putting a little money aside for unexpected expenses.

Shortly after starting my job at the doctor's office, I had a small fire in my clothes dryer at home. Fortunately, it was self-contained, quickly extinguished, and there was no damage to anything else. Because I had just started working the two jobs, I was getting caught up on some things after having been out of work for so long and then only working part-time for another five months. Now the dryer needed to be replaced.

However, I was not too concerned at that point because it was nice weather outside and I could hang my clothes up in the back yard to dry for the spring and summer. When winter came around, then I would try to find a dryer at that time. I did not think to pray and ask for a dryer at that point, knowing God knew what I needed and would provide as He already had for so many other needs I had. I actually enjoyed hanging clothes outside for a change. Besides, it would save on my electric bill.

The warm and hot season here in Georgia is quite long, so there were several months to go yet before I needed to start looking for a dryer. About three months after the fire, my pastor asked me out of the blue if I happened to need a washer and dryer. Only one person knew what had happened besides my family back home so there was no way possible he would have known about this particular need. I told him I needed a dryer because mine had quit working. I also decided to take the washer because mine was getting old and I did not know how much longer it would last. This set was almost brand new and had come out of a smoke-damaged house but never even smelled like smoke. They both still looked and worked like new! Some guys from the church came over to set them up for me. They also told me there would be no charge for the appliances! Like I mentioned before, God knows what we need even before we ask Him and He faithfully provides for ALL of His children's needs.

After working several months in the doctor's office, I was given the opportunity to work there on the days I was not needed at the hospital too, which helped a great deal financially. I was cross-trained in several areas of the office so I learned a lot of new skills. I grew to love this job as much as my transcription job and eventually I even started to do some of his office transcription as well.

We all became like family and I am so grateful that God led me to both of those jobs. They were definitely worth the wait! Like the ladies in my

Bible study had prayed for many months, I found more than just a job! I found a new secure career path where I could use my education and learn new skills too. I knew there would be a future with potential advancement with this new career path, which was not possible at my previous jobs. This job was also a much better fit for my interests and abilities, so instead of going to work frustrated like I used to, I had peace. It was a great feeling going to a job I enjoyed and best of all having a supportive Christian "family" who encouraged and prayed for each other. I know I could have called on any of them at any time of the day or night and they would have been there for me. I was incredibly blessed!

When you too are struggling through a long waiting period, remember that God has something wonderful waiting for you on the other side! Take advantage of that waiting period by drawing closer to Him. Seek His will for your life and ask Him what He would have you do and what He wants you to learn as you wait. Many times He uses these waiting periods to strengthen your character and grow your relationship with Him. He also wants to increase your faith in Him as He shows you His provision for every need as you wait, as He did in my case.

Most of all, remember that His timing is always perfect. Many times He is working a lot of things out behind the scenes that we cannot see to bring the end result to fruition. Sometimes He is preparing us for what is ahead because we are not ready for the blessing yet. Believe me, I know how difficult and frustrating it is to have to wait for months or even years for something I really want or need. I also know how hopeless these situations can seem at the time. But I can honestly say that through my waiting periods, God has developed my character and taught me to rest in Him and trust Him for the results…and see what He can do.

> *"Are not two sparrows sold for a penny? Yet not one of them will fall to the ground apart from the will of your Father. And even the very hairs of your head are numbered. So do not be afraid; you are worth more than many sparrows."*
> **Matthew 10:29-31**

CHAPTER 11

YAHWEH ROPHE
The LORD who Heals

It was like any other Thursday at work when I received a phone call from Joshua's school, stating that he had a bad headache preceded by a nosebleed and vomiting. As a mother, of course, I was concerned, but this was not out of the ordinary for him to have occasional nosebleeds that would make him sick, and he had always had his fair share of headaches. I asked if this was something they could give him an Ibuprofen for, and I would be there as soon as I could; however, it may be an hour before I could get there as it took over thirty minutes to get to the school from my job. They were insistent that I come and get him soon because he was really doing poorly and felt he needed to get home soon, so I left work immediately.

    I was not prepared for how bad it was until I got to the school. He was crying profusely like I had never seen him before. He said this was the worst headache he had ever had. I felt so bad for him and realized immediately that this was not a normal headache. It appeared to be a migraine, which he had never experienced before this time.

    I took him home, gave him Ibuprofen, a cold cloth, and put him in a darkened room because he said that any light or sound, even whispering, hurt his head even worse. Having experienced migraines myself, I knew what he was feeling, and I did everything I could to help make him comfortable.

I told him that if he still felt this bad the next day, I would take him to the pediatrician. I was fully expecting him to feel much better the next day because my migraines typically lasted twenty-four hours and then I felt fine. However, the next day he still had a headache just as bad as the day before, so I took him to the pediatrician. She sent us directly to the hospital emergency room because his vision was a little blurry and they could do more thorough testing there than she could in her office. We all thought at that point that it was just a typical migraine, but because this was his first one, the doctor wanted to get more thorough testing to make sure. Also, his vomit had a little blood in it, and that was cause for further concern.

As I walked Joshua into the ER, I noticed he started to have a hard time walking straight and I literally had to hold him up by putting my arms up under him. It was almost as if he were intoxicated by the way he was walking. He also stated that his vision was getting more blurry. Then, I noticed he began to slur his "s" sound which was not normal for him. At that point, I really got scared that this may possibly be more than just a migraine headache.

The hospital did a CAT scan and blood work, and both came back normal. After two rounds of different IV pain medications, his headache finally started to subside after a few hours, and he fell asleep. They then sent us home and told us to return should he become worse. He began to sleep a little better and slept most of the evening.

The next day, Saturday, he woke up and the "migraine" had come back. He was again in so much pain he was crying. I followed the same routine I did the previous two days by letting him lay in a quiet, dark room again. I prayed really hard for him the entire day that he would feel better because it was hard to see him in this much pain for so long. One of my biggest fears at that time was that he was going to struggle with these headaches chronically, and he would be confined to bed for days at a time, unable to function normally.

By late in the afternoon, I was beginning to think that something more than a migraine was going on, because of the severity of it and the fact that this headache had almost lasted for three days. I began to feel very uneasy about this, so I looked up directions to the children's hospital downtown, wrote them down and put them in my purse so I would know how to get there just in case I needed to take him. I was determined to get to the bottom of this, especially if he woke up feeling bad again the next day. I did not feel that the first hospital did much for him, so I was planning on taking him right to the children's hospital the next morning if he had not improved by then.

The next morning, Sunday, he woke up and said he felt fine. I was ecstatic that his head finally felt better after this three-day ordeal! He said he felt good enough to get out and go to church. I decided to take him even though he still did not look back to "normal." His eyelids and face were swollen and pale in color, but he assured me he felt much better and really wanted to go to church. So we went, and I kept a very close eye on his every move to make sure nothing was the least bit out of the ordinary with him.

"Coincidentally," that Sunday we had a healing service at church. A young lady first sang a song called, "The Healer Song," which made me cry like a baby. I was a bundle of emotions over the previous three days and it all came pouring out the moment I heard that song. Afterwards, the pastor asked for those who needed physical healing to come up to the altar to be anointed; I did not even hesitate to immediately take Joshua up front. He questioned why I was taking him up there when he said he felt better; I said to him, "If something is still going on, then being anointed for physical healing is what you need right now." Although I was very relieved that the headache was gone, part of me felt that something else was also going on because of how pale and swollen his face looked.

I am a big believer in being anointed for physical healing. I, too, have been anointed for constant migraines I had while pregnant with Joshua, and it took them almost completely away during the remainder of my pregnancy. I have also seen first-hand accounts of others being anointed and healed from various physical problems; therefore, I knew that he could be healed immediately from these headaches.

The rest of the day, Joshua kept busy working on little projects, and even played outside, so he seemed to be getting back to normal though I continued to keep a close eye on him for any changes. Other than his paleness, slightly swollen eyes and him moving slowly and lethargically, he looked and behaved basically the same as before this headache began.

He was very excited for the next day, Monday, because he was going to get to see his dad after school, who lived out of state and "coincidentally" was in town for work that weekend. I knew I would be able to determine how he truly felt by the way he behaved on Monday because he had something to really look forward to, and I know that when kids are excited about something, they suddenly feel much better.

Shortly after 5:15 a.m. the next morning, I was still asleep when Joshua came into my room, which was highly unusual for him although he does sometimes sleepwalk. The opening door startled me and I woke up, asking him if he was okay and he said, "Yes, Mama, I'm fine," and laid down next to me. Again, this was highly unusual for him, but I knew we had to get up soon anyway, and I was so exhausted I could barely talk, so I let him crash next to me. In every way he appeared to be fine and not in any pain.

I fell back into a deep sleep almost immediately and had a nightmare that a huge tornado was chasing me and the boys. We were outside in a field running towards a cellar. I was yelling back at the boys to hurry up because the tornado was catching up fast, and it seemed they were lagging further behind me. The dream terrified me to the point that I woke up and was unable to stay asleep for more than a few minutes at a time, although my eyes felt very heavy and I was completely exhausted. I now know by looking back that this was God's way of keeping me awake just enough to be aware of the upcoming "storm" about to take place.

About thirty minutes later, Joshua started kicking me and waking me up with each kick, which was really irritating. I nudged him with my foot and said, "Joshua, quit kicking me. You keep waking me up." He settled down for a few minutes, and then all of the sudden, he kicked forcefully and shook the bed violently. I thought at first he was just messing around, so I nudged him again, this time hard, with my foot and said his name. He did not respond, and a few seconds later, I knew something was really wrong; it appeared he may have been having a bad seizure. He had never had one before, nor had anyone in my family. It terrified me, because of the fact he had just had this bad migraine for three days and now this! I threw the covers off of him and ran to the light switch in order to see exactly what was happening. Nothing prepared me for what I saw when I turned on the lights.

He was very rigid and his neck was jerking backwards violently. His eyes were rolled back into his head and there was blood coming from both sides of his mouth. I yelled out to Jesus as loud as I could get out, "Lord Jesus, PLEASE DON'T LET HIM DIE LIKE THIS!!!" It looked to me as if he were dying right in front of me. I quickly checked his ears to see if there was blood coming out from them as well, but fortunately they were clean.

I ran out to the living room, grabbed the phone and dialed 911, so choked up I could barely squeak out a single word. I had to over-compensate by yelling into the phone to explain what was happening. I was very impatient because the operator could not understand me when telling her my address (because I was shaking so badly). Everything at that point seemed like a dream. It also felt as if somebody had their hands around my throat, squeezing so hard that I found it hard to breathe or talk.

After I got off the phone with 911, I ran into David's room to wake him up and tell him that Joshua had just had a seizure and the ambulance was on its way. While running towards his room, a voice told me "You HAVE to hold it together for David's sake!" This was absolutely essential to keep me from scaring him too, as he tended to get really scared during intense situations, and this would be the last thing we needed in that situation. It was definitely not by my own power but only with God's help that I was even able to remain calm enough, if only for a minute, to relay this message to David.

The seizure lasted a good five or six minutes, and when it finally stopped, I was unable to wake Joshua up. He was breathing very, very loudly and abnormally, as if mechanically by a machine. Blood was still coming out of his mouth. I desperately wanted it to stop and for him to wake up so I would know that he was all right. At this point, I still did not hear the sirens. I *again* dialed 911 and demanded to know where they were. It seemed like forever since I had made the first call. What was taking so long? The fire station was only four miles away!!??

I then ran outside with the phone in my hand, looking and listening for the ambulance. As the operator was checking on their location for me, I saw them turn down my street and told her I saw them and flagged them down. I was shaking so badly at that point it felt like I was going to jump out of my skin!

When the paramedics got to Joshua, they called his name multiple times and gently shook him to try and get a response from him. About fifteen minutes had elapsed since the seizure ended. When he finally regained consciousness, he sat up and opened his eyes really wide, like a deer in headlights. Then Joshua started to speak a little, but he was very confused and did not know what had happened, where he was or why all of these people were around him.

The paramedics finally took him out to the ambulance for transport to the hospital. Then I locked up and David and I went outside, only to find the ambulance still sitting on the street. Why had they not even left yet? I looked in the front seat; nobody was there. I looked in the back to see why they were still there and two EMT's were gently and patiently trying to calm him down so they could get the IV in his arm. He hated needles, and his eyes were huge as he pleaded with them not to stick him. They opened up the back door for me once they got the IV in, and I gave Joshua a kiss and told him I would meet them at the children's hospital downtown. Joshua later said he did not remember any of that happening. I was relieved that I was already prepared by having directions in my purse so I could find my way there.

I know that it was only by the grace of God and His watchful eye on my family that Joshua even came into my room shortly before this happened. Had he been in his own loft bed when this happened, he quite possibly could have fallen out and injured himself. It was also possible that we may not have even known exactly what had happened at all, because he did not remember any of it. Had I not known about the seizure, he may not have received the emergency medical care he needed until his condition progressed even further.

David and I headed to the children's hospital ER, even though it was a huge week for him at school due to state academic testing, and he was told that he absolutely could not miss school. Miraculously, I was able to reach his father at 6:30 a.m., who happened to be in town for work. I told him what had happened, and he met me at the emergency room. After they stabilized Joshua, Jake took David to school on his way back to work.

He said he would pick up David from school after work and take him to dinner; I was to let him know when we got home that evening or if they had decided to admit Joshua.

I also called Joshua's school's administrator. His school is a small, tight-knit private school so I called to make them aware of the situation and ask them to pray for Joshua. At the time I called, I did not know the administrator was out of town for a school event; however, he said he would immediately call the school to let them know the news and to pray for Joshua first thing, even before classes started. It really touched me that the entire school would pause before starting classes to pray for him by name! The school administrative staff and teachers kept in close contact throughout the day to check on his progress and to remind me they were praying for him. What a huge blessing this "extended family" was during those entire three days of his hospitalization! I know that without a doubt those prayers were what got us through the very emotionally difficult first day!

The fact that so many things "happened" to fall into place and were already taken care of ahead of time was nothing short of God's loving hand orchestrating everything into place for me. Although I already know that God sees everything we need ahead of time, it still truly amazes me even to this day whenever I think of the ways He goes about working things out!

While Joshua was still sleeping in the emergency room and we were waiting for blood work results to come back, I started prayer chains all around the country. Besides calling the school, I called my dad and stepmom and asked them to pray and put him on their prayer chain at church. I also called my aunt Jane, who lives next door to my mom, because initially I could not reach my mom. I called my supervisor at work to let her know what had happened and asked her to pass it on and pray for him, too. Later, I put a prayer request on Facebook so that my out-of-state friends and family could be updated and pray for him.

Joshua was still sedated from the IV medications they gave him, but when he finally did come out of it a little, he said his head again hurt a lot, like it did for those three days the week before, so they gave him pain medication to help that too. I was very glad that at least he had the chance to see his dad one of those times he was awake in between sleeping.

We sat in the emergency room for about an hour or two before my stomach started to feel sick from having not eaten anything all morning combined with the stress of the situation. I did not want to leave Joshua's side for even a minute to find something to eat, but I did not want to get really sick either by not eating anything, which would have literally kept me in the bathroom for much of the morning and not with him.

About 15 minutes later, this total stranger came into the emergency room, walked right up to me, and gave me a big bear hug. She introduced herself as someone who attended the church where Joshua's school is located and said that the pastor of the church, also the school administrator, had called and asked her to come by and see us because she worked at that hospital in the offices. She prayed with me and asked if there was anything she could get me to eat and drink, which was a huge blessing! She came back a few minutes later with breakfast and a bottled water. The Lord saw and took care of my needs at just the right moment through this "angel."

With my family so far away from here, I felt very alone before this "angel" walked in. Although I was comforted by the fact that prayer chains were starting, I still wished for a familiar face to sit with us. Even though this lady was unknown to me before this point, I was extremely comforted by her presence at that moment.

After about another hour, they decided to admit Joshua as his blood work results were starting to come back abnormal. His blood pressure was also very high even for an average person, and his blood pressure normally ran a little low. As they were wheeling him up to the room, his youth pastor got there and walked up to the room with us and prayed with us before he left. It was comforting to see a familiar face at that moment.

In order to get his blood pressure under control, investigate why this happened and to determine which other parts of his body were affected, they had to run a lot of other tests that would take at least another day to run and get the results back on. The first test they ordered was an echocardiogram, which took quite a while to get done. There were two techs performing this test, and at first it appeared to them there was a problem with his heart; however, before they left they said they could not find anything serious but that the cardiologist would have to read the test to be sure.

The future was so uncertain at this point, and I kept praying that God would send just the right doctors to help Joshua and give them the wisdom to find out quickly what had caused all of these acute problems. I was very shaken yet, somehow, able to remain calm enough at the same time on the outside because I knew that God was in control of this situation, and when we did find out the results, God would see us through it. This is what we call the "peace that passes all understanding," when your world feels like it's falling apart all around you, and everything is uncertain, but yet, you feel His presence and peace with you every step of the way.

Later that day, they did an MRI of his brain and ran some more blood work. I was told that his urine had high levels of blood and protein in it. They also noted that his blood pressure continued to spike, until it reached 216/130 at its highest. The nurse on duty told me that this was the blood pressure of an old man ready to have a heart attack or stroke, and that was probably the scariest moment for me!! However, I was reassured by the fact that we were at one of the best children's hospitals, that they would find the problem and that Joshua would be closely monitored.

The first MRI was not very clear because he moved a bit during the test, and they had to redo it the next morning under sedation. The next morning, along with the MRI, they did a kidney scan and an EEG. I did not think the kidneys had much to do with this problem at first, so I was confused as to why they were looking so closely at them. I was more focused on his head, the seizure, and the neurological symptoms and did not think of the other areas that had possibly been affected.

A tech in the kidney ultrasound department noted that one of his kidneys was quite large, and the other one was slightly enlarged. She verified again how old he was because it was highly unusual to see someone of his age and size to have such a big kidney. That also concerned me because I knew something was going on with his blood pressure and head, and now there was a problem with his kidneys. I could not wait to finally talk to a doctor to answer the list of mounting questions I had.

The rest of that day, Tuesday, was very difficult for Joshua because he started to feel better and said he did not think he needed to have all of these tests done. He said he was fine and just wanted to go home…right now! It made me smile a bit, knowing my Joshua was back and he was still the same person as before the seizure happened. He did not understand that even though he felt a little better, there were still a lot of things going on inside of him that needed to be figured out yet before he could go home. The worst part of the testing was the EEG and waiting for the tech to get all of those little electrodes placed just right on the head of a kid that did NOT want to be there. That was one of the longest thirty minutes of my life!

Test after test was being done the entire day, yet I still had no definite answers and was told the neurologist would not be there to see me until first thing the next morning to talk to me about the MRI findings. Though it was still hard to sleep that night, I had a deeper sense of peace than I had felt since all of this happened which I believe was due to all of the prayers going up for him as word got out about his condition. I also noticed my stomach was no longer in knots that second day.

That day, one of Joshua's friends called my cell phone. Joshua had been invited to this friend's birthday party that Saturday, and he was calling to see if he was coming because I had not been able to RSVP. I told him Joshua was in the hospital, and I was not sure if he would be better by Saturday. His mother called me back within five minutes after we had hung up, after her son told her what had happened to Joshua. She asked if there was anything she could do to help me. I thanked her and said I would be in touch and let her know. She said they would keep him in their prayers and really hoped he could make it to her son's birthday party because the two boys had been friends since second grade, and her son really wanted Joshua to feel better so that he could come. Because the boys were now at different schools, they had not been able to spend as much time together as they had before.

That evening, Jake brought David back up to the hospital and said he had to leave town the next morning; he could not take David to school the next day. I was hoping that maybe he would stay in town a little longer, at least until Joshua was discharged. I started to fret because I was not about to leave Joshua there alone to drive thirty minutes each way for any reason, even to take David to school when I still did not have many answers yet concerning Joshua's condition. Also, my dog needed to be fed and let outside in the evening and first thing in the morning. Their dad agreed to stay at the hospital with Joshua while I ran home, took a shower, let the dog out and packed a few clothes for me and Joshua.

As soon as I got back to the hospital, I called Joshua's friend's mom back and asked if she could come and pick up David, have him stay the night with them, take him to school in the morning (her daughter went to the same school), and let my dog out and feed her too. She was happy to help me out by driving the thirty-minute trip each way to pick up David and take care of him and the dog.

Again, God saw the needs and provided the means to take care of another potential problem that came up along the way. Though she lives close to my house, I would not have even thought to ask for her help had it not been for her son calling us about his birthday party.

So many people say the cliché, "Let me know if you need anything," but very few will actually go out of their way to help when a big need arises. However, this sister in Christ actually went the extra mile to help us, and that is what being a follower of Christ means. That act alone would have changed my life had I been an unbeliever. Actions speak much louder than words by showing people how much you really care.

We have been blessed with two wonderful church families (our home church and the church at Joshua's school) that called us throughout the three days he was hospitalized. A few of them even stopped by to visit, among them his favorite teacher! One of his other teachers brought him a goodie bag full of treats and get-well notes written by each of his classmates. It was very touching and thoughtful!

On Wednesday morning, we finally got some test results. I first spoke with the pediatric neurologist, who came into the room with a look that immediately told me he had found something on the MRI that was not good news. Again, I believed that God had this whole situation under control and in His hands, and that he would give us the strength to get through this no matter how bad the news was.

The neurologist said that, of course, there were a few possibilities of what the problem was for sure, but he strongly suspected a condition called RPLS (reversible posterior leukoencephalopathy syndrome), which affects the white matter in the brain, causing it to swell. This is also known as capillary leak syndrome. Fortunately, in Joshua's case, it was the reversible type. The other type, which is non-reversible, can cause brain dysfunction, permanent neurologic deterioration, kidney failure and even death in some cases. He also assured me that this was not a seizure disorder and most likely he would not have another seizure. I was very relieved to find out it was reversible and that it was not a seizure disorder. I was told that it should only take a few weeks, or in the worst case scenario up to a month, to heal. Now I knew that the headache he had was not only a migraine but an actual problem going on in his brain.

Not only were his brain and blood pressure affected, his kidneys were as well. With his blood pressure being abnormally high, it affected his kidneys and he was dropping blood and protein in his urine. A pediatric nephrologist came in and explained that he also had a particular type of nephritis, a chronic inflammation of the kidneys, which is sometimes associated with slow, progressive loss of kidney function. They were enlarged, not filtering correctly and his creatinine levels were very high. The serum complements (proteins) in his kidneys were very low as well, which could possibly indicate some kidney failure.

The immediate course of treatment was to bring down and stabilize his blood pressure with medication and put him on a low-sodium diet. This would, in turn, start to help his kidneys return to normal again. He would have to follow up with the nephrologist in a few weeks to have more blood drawn to see if his kidneys were beginning to return to normal or not.

On that Wednesday afternoon, the nurse told me they were going to discharge Joshua later that afternoon. Because I knew he was stable and about ready to leave, I ran home to pick up David from school and brought him back to the hospital. However, when I returned an hour later, the nurse told me his blood pressure went back up again and he could not leave until it was stabilized. I thought we were so close to being able to take him home and everything was improving, but another setback occurred, which really upset me. I did not know how much longer he would have to stay now, or if his blood pressure going back up again could possibly cause another chain reaction to occur, bringing about another seizure. Fortunately, after a few more hours his blood pressure stabilized, and we were able to start the discharge process.

Joshua was released around dinner time, on the same day as David's birthday. Joshua said he was up to going out to dinner, so we went out and celebrated David's birthday and the fact that Joshua was now out of the hospital.

I was very grateful to God that they found the problem fairly quickly and knew what had to be done in order to begin reversing it! I thanked Him over and over that He answered my prayers so quickly by bringing the right team of doctors together who worked very hard to put all of the pieces together and come up with a diagnosis and treatment plan to help him recover; though it seemed at the time to take forever to get the answers.

Shortly after being discharged from the hospital, Joshua asked me why he had the seizure in the first place when he had just been anointed the day before it happened. I assured him that even though we do not see the whole picture, God does, and it was very possible that this could have turned out far worse than it did by being the non-reversible type of RPLS, for instance. I am still convinced that things would not have turned out as well as they did had God's anointing touch not been upon him that Sunday.

All of these problems he experienced – the seizure, brain capillary leak, headache, dangerously high blood pressure, and kidney problems – were post-infectious complications from the strep throat he had three weeks prior to the seizure.

The week after Joshua was discharged from the hospital, he went back to school and I went back to work. Every day I drove past this particular church on my way to work that had a flashing sign in front with the temperature, time and various short messages. For the entire first week that I was back at work, that sign flashed MY name along with "Jesus loves you" every time I drove by it, whether in the morning or on my way home. I have never seen a church sign flash my name on it before that point.

I do not think it coincidental that I cried out to JESUS specifically the week before to not let my son die, and for that sign to say to me, "JESUS loves you." God works in mysterious ways, too many to count. I emailed the pastor of that church and told him what had happened and how that message spoke to me, and he actually emailed me back! I was not expecting that because I was someone off the street he had never even met before, but he took the time to write me a nice email in response. Just over a year later, the Lord led us to start attending that church, and we have been blessed in countless ways by following His lead there. He truly never ceases to completely amaze me!!!

Two weeks after his discharge, Joshua had to follow up with the nephrologist (kidney doctor). He also had to follow up with his pediatrician on a weekly basis for the next month or so to closely monitor his blood pressure and urine. Although the hospital discharged Joshua with a two-week prescription for Norvasc to control his blood pressure, he had to remain on it much longer, as his blood pressure stayed up longer than they anticipated. About four months later, he was finally able to come off of the Norvasc, much longer than the projected two or three weeks. At that time, he could also gradually begin to work in small amounts of sodium to his diet.

That summer we practically lived at the pediatrician's office; I was considering moving in temporarily because we were always there anyway. By the time the summer had ended, I was counting my blessings that the pediatrician staff remained totally professional and genuinely patient with us, (even though Joshua was not always cooperative, to say the least).

I also had the privilege of working for a doctor and his wife who were supportive and encouraging during that time. They never once complained that I had to be at the doctor's office so much with my son that summer, and they checked on me frequently that week he was in the hospital and told me they were praying for him. I did not have the added burden of possibly losing my job due to these absences, which allowed me to focus all my energy and time on helping my son recuperate. I know there are a lot of employers who would not have been as merciful.

When he went back to the nephrologist for his kidney follow up visit, recent blood results came back and his kidney levels were still not within normal limits. He still had protein and blood in his urine as well, which concerned her because she said those levels should have all returned to normal by that point if those problems were, in fact, caused by post-strep complications. However, she was not as concerned about the blood in his urine because that could remain for up to a full year. Because the complement levels in his kidneys were still abnormal, there was now the possibility that this was another problem we were dealing with.

She wanted him to return again in another six weeks or so to have his blood redrawn. If the serum complement levels in the kidneys were back to normal by that time, then it simply meant that it just took him longer to recover from the post-infectious nephritis. However, if the levels were not back to normal by then, the problem was not from post-infectious complications. If this were the case, she would most likely have to do a kidney biopsy to find out what was causing the problem.

Eight weeks later we went back and had his blood redrawn, and she tested his urine for protein and blood again. She said the urine was finally free of protein but still had quite a bit of blood in it. We had to wait a few days for the blood results to see what they showed before we did anything further. When the results came back, one of the serum complement levels was almost back to normal, but the other one was still quite abnormal. Based on this information, she concluded that he has a C3 complement deficiency (which will make him more susceptible to bacterial infections) and glomerulonephritis, inflammation of the structures in the kidney that produce urine. There is not much they can do for these, only keep an eye on his blood and urine once or twice a year and if he has any unusual symptoms, have his kidneys rechecked.

Since that time, Joshua has had no more complications or reoccurrences. Not only that, but he has actually been sick from infections LESS often than before all of this happened! I am so grateful to YAHWEH ROPHE, the God who healed my son!

"Is any one of you sick? He should call the elders of the church
To pray over him and anoint him with oil in the name of the Lord.
And the prayer offered in faith will make the sick person well;
The Lord will raise him up."
James 5:14-15

CHAPTER 12

A Year of Rest, Blessing and Preparation

The Lord began me on a year-long journey which started in November, 2011, preparing me for perhaps one of the greatest trials of my life. Although He has spoken to me countless times before, this time was different. He was speaking very intently, constantly, and clearly. After the third specific message He gave me, I felt He was trying to tell me something much bigger. For this reason, I thought it important to begin writing everything down so I could begin to put the pieces together to be able to see the bigger picture.

DECEMBER 2011

The following words from the Lord came to me unmistakably loud and clear: "Rest your body (and rest in me)." It has always been difficult for me to relax and take a break, because I grew up in a home where rest was wrong, frowned upon and considered pure laziness. For this reason, I have always been a very hard worker. Eventually, this took a toll on my body after several years. This besides the fact that there is always so much to have to get done as a single parent, and at this particular time, I was working three part-time jobs.

However, at this particular season in my life, God was telling me to rest my body, both physically and mentally. I have learned over the past several years as a single parent that when God asks me to do something, there is a specific reason for it even if it does not make sense or seem possible to do.

Therefore, I began to make a conscious effort to rest, asking for His help in doing just that because it would not be easy for me to do in my own strength for obvious reasons. Shortly afterwards, my favorite song artist *David Crowder Band* released their final album rightly named, "Give Us Rest." It was a very bittersweet moment as my favorite artist, whose music had really ministered to me for several years, was no longer going to be ministering through music. The name of the album, however, reaffirmed what God was asking me to do. The timing could not have been more perfect; this was definitely a "God thing!"

Besides telling me to rest, the Lord reminded me that my hope is in HIM...alone. Although I already knew and believed this, I needed to be reminded again (particularly for this upcoming trial) that my hope is not in my circumstances, others or even myself, but ONLY in Him. He also reassured me that it is okay to slow down and rest, *because* my hope is in Him.

Around this particular time the song, "My Hope is in You" by Aaron Shust spoke volumes to me as it confirmed this. I began hearing this song three or four times every day on the radio – too much to be merely coincidence. The chorus states, "My hope is, in You Lord/All the day long/I won't be shaken by drought or storm/A peace that passes understanding is my song/And I sing, My hope is, in you Lord."[1]

Early January 2012

The Lord was asking me to do something else very, very difficult, which was to "Praise Me even through (in the midst of) the storms." I must say that it takes everything within me to even smile or laugh during a really rough time. The rougher the time, the harder it is, let alone being able to push past all of the difficulties and praise God anyway. In my case, it's more like "hold on for dear life and ask God to give me the strength to survive through the trial intact and help me to learn what He is teaching me in the process." Obviously, this was a skill He needed to refine in me, and I could ONLY do this with His strength working in this area of great weakness in my life.

One Sunday in particular, I had just come through a *very* difficult week all around where everything seemed to happen at once; kids misbehaving more than usual, unexpected financial stresses, etc. However, I was very determined that this time was going to be different because of what the Lord had just spoken to my heart about praising Him in spite of those things. Even though I could not stop crying throughout the entire service, I decided to push past the emotions with everything that I had and sing my praises to God, because He still deserved every bit of praise I could possibly give Him. I sang out each song with all my heart to an audience of one, tears and all, feeling shattered on the inside but determined to give the God that I love all the praise, despite how I felt.

Something amazing happened through that. I had a breakthrough moment that I welcomed with open arms and so greatly needed. I felt an amazing peace wash over me for the rest of that day in the middle of some very overwhelming situations because I gave God my best praise through it. That moment left an impression on me that I will never forget; when we praise God and bless His name in our **most difficult moments,** we are truly blessed because it was a sacrifice of praise. It sure is easy to praise God when things are going well, but not as easy when everything around us screams "disaster" and we have to push past the difficulties to praise Him from the bottom of our hearts.

February 2012

Shortly after this breakthrough, in February 2012, I had some x-rays done of my neck and spine. At this time, I was getting very concerned about some progressing weakness, tremors, and stiffness in my neck and back along with all-over numbness and tingling over the previous two years and my doctor wanted to find the cause. The results came back showing that I had spurs (painful bony growths that develop when vertebrae wear down from degeneration/arthritis) growing on my neck and spine along with a bulging disc in my neck. She ordered an MRI to see how serious it was and if there were any other problems with my spine that could be causing these multiple symptoms.

Being the researcher that I am, I started looking into what I could do to help relieve the pain I began experiencing in my neck. The answer I found rang loud and clear; the best thing to do for this type of pain was to rest. That is exactly what the Lord had just told me to do a few months prior to this! He knew all along what I needed to be doing to help my body heal even before I knew what was wrong! And, unlike me, God did **not** need Google to come up with the answer!

This little setback did not keep my focus off of listening intently for God to speak to me again in preparation for my upcoming trial. He certainly did not skip a beat as He, in the midst of all of this, spoke again. I love how God speaks in so many ways, too many ways to count and often in ways we do not expect. He quietly whispered to my spirit that, "I never let go (even if you cannot hang on)." A confirmation and reminder of this was through another David Crowder Band song, "Never Let Go." To my knowledge, they had not played that song on my station before that point (nor have they since then); however, it played on the radio just a day or two afterwards. A few lines of the song state, "...Ever faithful, ever true/You I know...You never let go. Oh what love, oh, what love...In joy and pain/In sun and rain...You're the same/Oh, You never let go."[2] Only our amazing Creator, who knows us so well, could speak this powerfully through music.

This gentle reminder brought to the front of my mind what I already knew, but needed to hear again; that He is the **same**, no matter how rough and dark things would get in my life. Even if everything felt like it had changed around me, He stays constant. His love does not change; He will not give up on me nor will He let go of me when I need Him most. The same God that has helped me before will help me again. Even though I may change during the difficult seasons of life, He will not.

Just as importantly, when I am at my happiest, He is there rejoicing with me. When I am at my lowest, He is there broken with me. Even if all the people I considered friends left my side through my broken seasons, God would not leave me because He never leaves our side; He never changes. It has often been said that the true mark of a friend is shown by how they respond when things get really difficult in your life. Either they stick by your side with you through the trials, encouraging you and praying with you and for you, or they suddenly disappear. Although some of those whom I considered good "friends" backed away from me and were very unsupportive during that trial (and it hurt deeply), God blessed me with a small handful of friends who, when this trial did come into my life months later, were there for me through all of it. Their prayers and encouragement were an important lifeline for me as I was going through the most difficult year of my life. God Himself is that kind of friend as well, even if at the time we may not feel Him near.

Shortly after the results of my x-rays came back, the Lord spoke to my spirit the words, "I'm still Healer." As is usually the case, He confirmed this over and over everywhere I turned; during my personal devotions, Scriptures I read, the radio, and sermons all spoke of God as Healer, reminding me that He is STILL in the healing business. I already knew this, of course, but when God goes out of His way to remind me of something this much, there is a reason for it. He needed me to keep this in the very front of my mind. I had a gut feeling they were going to find something wrong on the MRI that I was about to have done, but of course this would not be a problem too big for God to heal!

A few weeks later, I got the results of the MRI, which showed three moderate to severe spinal problems besides the herniated disc. Along with that, they found three lesions on my brain which were consistent nine times out of ten with Multiple Sclerosis. I was taken aback by the news as that was the last thing I was expecting to explain the multiple, slowly progressing neurological problems I had over the previous two-and-a-half years. I had always been extremely healthy and never had a test result come back abnormal for anything before. Though I was initially taken aback and even shed tears with this news, I also had a deep sense of peace that let me know this was going to be okay no matter the outcome. I knew that God would be with me and that some type of healing would take place as He reminded me right beforehand that He is "still in the healing business." Because of this, I was able to maintain my composure upon hearing this news.

March 2012

By early March I developed a quickly progressing weakness in both legs, to the point that I either had to pull myself up by grabbing onto something or push myself up out of a chair using all of the strength in my arms in order to stand up. This happened over a period of about a month and was a scary time for me. It was becoming harder to walk between my two jobs across the parking lot from each other as I had previously done with no problems.

I took the first opportunity I had during this time to have my pastor pray over me and anoint me with oil for healing. Although we did not have a 100% firm diagnosis of MS at this point, the symptomatology and the initial series of tests were strongly pointing to that diagnosis, so I had him pray for MS. (Several other diagnoses had already been ruled out by this time). The **very next day**, the quickly progressing weakness and pain in my legs was 100% gone! It was like nothing had ever gone wrong with my legs! I had absolutely no trouble walking or standing to my feet normally. To this day, I thank God that I can walk and stand up normally without any assistance, and I learned not to take those things for granted anymore!

April 2012

In the month of April, the Lord asked me a very surprising question, "Do you trust Me?" Over the previous eight years as a single parent, I have had to trust Him over and over for everything. It was rare to find myself not trusting Him because He had come through for me so many times in so many ways that I really had no reason NOT to trust Him. My first thought was to wonder why He was asking me the obvious. However, after pondering this a while, I thought, "What if my house burned down and I lost everything I had or lost one or both of my kids? Could I still trust Him?" Truthfully, I was not sure I could if something catastrophic were to happen, so I asked God to help me trust Him even more!

God did not ask me that question because He did not know the answer; rather, He needed for me to realize that I fully trusted Him only to a certain point. Although I have felt over the past eight years that my level of trust in Him has been great, I only truly needed to fully trust Him in the areas I had already experienced. I needed to expand my trust in Him for things I had not yet experienced, where everything depended on my level of trust in Him.

June 6, 2012

Again, God was speaking to me as YAHWEH ROPHE (Healer). I had reached a section in my devotional book at this point on Jesus' healing ministry. As I went through day one, then days two, three and four of devotions relating to Jesus' healings, I decided to go through the gospels and find every record of physical healing and write down how each person was healed and the circumstances around each healing. A common theme throughout was that Jesus healed based on the person's level of faith. In many cases, He also physically touched them, or they physically touched Him.

God had already begun healing my body physically, and I believed that He would finish what He started no matter what the doctors found after the remaining tests were done to determine if this was in fact Multiple Sclerosis. Throughout the previous two years, weakness in my entire left side was progressing as were the tremors, which by this point had now moved into my right hand as well as to my core. Over the past year, I also began to have falls, episodes of slurred speech, increased problems with balance, and blurred vision several times a day along with increasing nerve pain. There are now some days when I feel very fatigued, among other problems. Although at times it feels like my physical body is losing control and malfunctioning, I have peace knowing that this is not too big for God to heal and there is hope beyond this, because my hope is in Him and He still heals today!

JUNE 20, 2012

"Do not fear the unknown." The Lord was reassuring me by reminding me very clearly not to fear what was to come. The first thing I heard that very morning as I woke up to the radio was that the Bible says the words "FEAR NOT" or "DO NOT FEAR" 365 times, one time for each day of the year! After hearing this, it was clear to me that God was making a strong statement here about fear!

I was coming into a season where I was being prepared again and again for a big trial coming up and I admit that I was fearful of what that was going to mean for my life. What would I lose? What would happen? Would my family be okay? Would something happen to completely turn my world upside down? In the midst of all these difficult questions, all I could do was ask God to help me have the strength, courage and fearlessness I would need to make it through whatever was coming.

Typically, I am not a fearful person in my normal day-to-day life and would even venture to say I am fearless in many circumstances where others tend to be afraid. However, this was uncharted territory I was about to enter, and I knew that if the Lord was preparing me this long for something, it was going to be big! That being said, I had fear of the unknown "giant" coming my way, and I often recited my favorite Bible verse, **II Timothy 1:7**, which says, "For God hath not given us a spirit of fear, but of power, and of love and of a sound mind." (KJV)

August 23, 2012

I was barely even awake at 6:00 a.m. on this particular day, when suddenly a prayer came clearly to my mind. I immediately grabbed a pen and paper and wrote it down, as it was too good to forget.

"Lord, grant me the strength to have a smile on my face, joy in my heart and glorify your name through this trial (so that others may see you in me through this)." I kept this prayer posted on my mirror where I would see it every day and set that as a personal goal for when the time came.

September 20, 2012

Due to the doctor retiring for whom I had worked the past four years, I was having to apply for another job.

My first interview for a particular job I really wanted was a disaster. I went into the interview sure that I would do great, as it was for the same type of job I had been doing for the previous four years. However, they handed me a thick stack of papers stapled together and said that this "written test" was only part one of the interview. As I started reading through the questions, my heart began to sink. It seemed like for every five answers I knew, there were five I did not know. What was even more frustrating was the fact that I did know many of the answers, but just blanked out and could not think of the right answer. However, I did the best I could and plowed through it hoping that despite how I felt about the test, (as I have always been a terrible test taker) it would work out in the end.

The next part of my interview consisted of listening to dictation from several different doctors (most of whom had very thick accents) and transcribing what I heard. I got through the first two fine but I still had two more to go. It became such a struggle that I finally stopped (knowing I was in over my head at that point) and said to the interviewer, "I'm sorry. I just do not think this will work out for me." It broke my heart to say that because I loved doing transcription and was good at it. However, I was told that for this job, I would have to transcribe every specialty (cardiology, neurology, oncology, etc.) for every type of foreign accent and stay on top of everything and do it well.

I left that interview feeling broken and defeated. Why was it so hard to get my mind to think straight these days, when I needed my mind to be sharp and clear for this period of time in my life? I left there in tears, embarrassed that I had done so poorly for an educated person with so much experience. When I got into the car, I started crying. I also prayed, asking God why things had to go so wrong for a job that seemed right for me. As soon as I regained my composure, I started the car and immediately a song came on the radio that said specifically, "don't give up, help is surely on the way…don't give up, the dark is breaking into day[3]…" It was like God was telling me to keep going and do not give up, because my new job was right around the corner…

Right before I went to interview for the next job, the Lord laid the verse **Jeremiah 29:11** on my heart, which reads, *"For I know the plans I have for you," declares the Lord, "plans to prosper you and not to harm you, plans to give you hope and a future."* (NIV)

I have always struggled with believing this verse was for people like me because even though I have always put 100% effort (and lots of prayer) into everything, my life has still been filled with one difficulty, struggle and failure after the other. Prosperity has been the last thing I had ever seen when it came to my life. However, here it was and the Lord was determined to make sure this verse came before me multiple times over a short period of time. Obviously, He was trying to tell me something.

A day or two before my next job interview, I woke up to a song artist talking on my radio station about Jeremiah 29:11 and how this verse had spoken to her during a very difficult time in her life. When I went in for this job interview, the room they put me in to wait for the interviewing doctor had Jeremiah 29:11 on the wall in front of me in big bold letters, clear as day. A few days after the interview, I was watching *700 Club* and there was some type of glitch and another segment from a different airing of the show came on and Gordon Robertson quoted, you guessed it, Jeremiah 29:11. Then he said a few things, and the show had another glitch and went back to the original show that was airing. I would not have believed this happened had I not seen it myself! It stopped me in my tracks, like the Lord was making every effort for me to know that He did have a plan for me and that I did have hope and a future, even through this very difficult season I was about to enter.

As hard as it had been at times to believe this verse applied to people like me, I could not deny it any longer. Things were beginning to heat up in my life at this point and it was becoming more difficult to believe I had any hope for a good future. Although it is still sometimes difficult for me to see that God has a good, prosperous future for me, I have chosen to believe it in faith alone though I cannot yet see His plan.

<u>Early October 2012</u>

We had a special healing service coming up at our church on October 6. Ever since I found out about the upcoming service, I declared that date as the day that God <u>would</u> heal my spine. By this point, getting comfortable enough to sleep was almost impossible. I had to use several pillows and blankets all around me just to try and find a somewhat comfortable spot to stop the severe pain and stiffness that had begun over the summer months. It had come to the point that my spine felt like the vertebrae had fused together. The stiffness was unbelievable, as if the spaces between my vertebrae were missing, which made turning and bending nearly impossible. It was very, very painful to turn over in bed. Laying on my left side, the side with the most severe spinal stenosis, was excruciating, unbearable, and just about impossible to do. However, I was <u>still going to declare in faith that</u> October 6 would be the day of healing for this excruciating pain and stiffness. God had already touched my legs and they were still going strong, so I knew He would continue His healing, and I could not wait for it!

The time came for the service, and I was prayed over for a healing touch on my spine. I had peace knowing that God was going to give me a brand new spine! I had <u>no doubt</u> in my mind whatsoever because I had already previously claimed that it was **already done.**

I left the service that night feeling the same physically, but I knew the healing was literally right around the corner. I went to bed that night and as usual, I woke up and changed positions in bed and the stiffness was 100% totally gone! I sat up, stood up, and bent over freely with absolutely no stiffness. The chronic, bitter pain from that point on was about 85% less than it had been previously and continued to get a little better each month after that! The difference between how I felt that night when I went to bed and when I woke up a few hours later was ASTRONOMICAL! It literally felt as if God went in and loosened up my vertebrae, making my spine flexible and normal again!

Because of the other spinal problems I have, I still continue to have some intense pain in my spine when I overdo it, yet I am much better off than I was before October 6, 2012. The chronic pain and stiffness is gone, and I can move and flex my back like I did years ago, as if nothing had ever happened. For this reason I am beyond grateful! There is no doctor or chiropractor on earth that can instantly touch and heal severe pain and stiffness like the Great Physician can, and I am going to keep believing in faith that God will finish the amazing work He has begun in my spine because I believe that my God finishes what He starts!

I believe that God radically healed me for two reasons. One, because I had faith not only that He COULD heal my spine but that He WOULD heal it! Many times Jesus said during His healing ministry that the one receiving the healing was healed because of his or her faith. For example, Luke 8:48 states, *"Daughter, your faith has healed you. Go in peace."* (NIV) Second, I believe He was trying to increase my faith in this area by this radical healing so I could look back and remember what He has already done in my body because I would need that for future reference.

I do realize that in some cases God chooses not to heal physically for reasons unknown to us. There will always be disease and illness in a broken world. Sometimes the process of the illness or disease brings Him more glory than the healing of it, and sometimes He even uses those things to draw us and those around us closer to Him to increase our trust in Him. Whatever the case may be, I do know that He can and does still heal today, many times in ways that leave doctors scratching their heads.

Late October 2012

I was referred to a new neurologist, who, after taking my history and reviewing my MRIs and blood work, stated that I needed to have a spinal tap done to either rule out or determine for sure whether I had Multiple Sclerosis or whether this was some other disease process. She said she could do nothing else for me unless I had this done so she could get to the root of the problem.

I am definitely not a fan of needles, especially giant ones, and initially I said "No way! I'm not getting that done!" Surely there were other tests she could run that could rule things out besides this, but she again told me that a spinal tap could rule out or determine the big things, and it needed to be done before she could proceed with other testing.

She decided to give me a few weeks to think about it and let her know at my next appointment what I wanted to do. At that point I was almost certain that I would not change my mind about this because I did not want a huge needle stuck in my back and risk the possible complications with that procedure. However, at that point I was at a crossroads. Either I could not get it done and not know with 100% certainty whether this was MS (as it continued to progress), or get it done and out of the way and then move forward with the treatment and go on with my life. The second choice sounded much better, but the fear of having the spinal tap really stood in the way. So, I did what I always did in situations when I needed wisdom; I prayed.

I fiercely prayed for wisdom on what to do because I knew that God knew whether or not I really needed this test done to find the problem or if there was another way without it. He already knew what the problem was, and I asked that He would give the doctor the wisdom to be able to find the problem. I also prayed that God would give me supernatural peace if this was the right route to go and there was absolutely no other way to find out the answer. I prayed, "Lord, if I need to get the spinal tap done, give me peace about it, but if not (and you already know if it is really necessary or not) do not let me have peace about it. I ask for the wisdom to know clearly what to do here."

The very next afternoon an overwhelming peace washed over me which reassured me that I needed to get this done. For the most part, the fear went away and at that moment I knew I needed to go ahead with the spinal tap even though a small part of me was still reluctant.

About six weeks later, I had the procedure done. I could feel the Lord's sweet presence in that room, which I particularly needed because the first thing the doctor said was, "this is going to be a complicated case." This was not reassuring, especially when she had a huge needle in her hand. However, I was able to keep calm for the most part.

She was right. The first time was a dry stick, which meant no spinal fluid came out. This meant she had to go back in again on the other side of my spine. On the way in, she hit a nerve that sent an electric shock through my body, and I jerked. She hit the same nerve on the way out. This also happened when she went in on the other side. By that point I was just praying that I would make it out of there with no permanent damage and be able to walk out normally. A few hours later, I walked out and was very relieved and thankful for the Lord's presence in that room, that the doctor was able to finally get some spinal fluid, and that I walked out without difficulty. However, I hope to never have to go through that very painful experience again!

All of the preceding events and months of God speaking very intently, purposefully and directly prepared me well for the fierce battle that lay ahead. Throughout the battle, I regularly reread my journal as I had written all of this down to refer to when the time came. I was going to be ready for anything…or so I thought. I would soon find out that it was going to be a more difficult battle than I ever imagined. I would never have made it through without all of the preparation the Lord had given me beforehand. Everything He had told me over the previous year had in some way given me just enough strength to make it through one more day, then one more week, then one more month.

> *"This is what the Lord says to you: 'Do not be afraid or discouraged because of this vast army. For the battle is not yours, but God's…Go out to face them tomorrow, and the Lord will be with you.'"*
> **II Chronicles 20:15b, 17b**

Chapter 13

The Battle Begins

"You (I)...are (am) from God and have overcome...because the one who is in you (me) is greater than the one who is in the world." **(I John 4:4)** (NIV) This is one of the verses I often claimed during the upcoming battle and it encouraged me when I was too weak to do anything else.

It started with a simple sinus infection along with a bad case of asthmatic bronchitis that lasted all of December and halfway into January. Even though I have always had exercise-induced asthma, this second case of asthmatic bronchitis made my asthma progress to the point that I now had full-blown asthma. I now had to use an inhaler twice every day just to keep from wheezing and coughing chronically.

When I went in for my asthmatic bronchitis appointment, I had to be prescribed a special type of inhaler because I had a skin reaction in the past to the one that was normally prescribed. However, I was told that it was over a hundred dollars per inhaler. Because it was an expensive and less often prescribed inhaler, the clinic I was going to (which was a ministry for the uninsured working class that charged you on a sliding scale based on income) said they would see if there were any donated samples available for me in the back. They did not have one, so I went to the pharmacy to pick one up. However, they said they did not have one available either and did not know how long it would take to get one in. I really needed one yesterday! Talk about being kicked while I was already down...

The pharmacist said to keep checking back over the next few days to see if they could get a donated inhaler for me. Every breath at this point was a struggle and the cough horrendous. I cried and prayed all the way home that God would provide an inhaler the next day; He knew my needs and knew how much I needed it. However, it was nerve-wracking not knowing how long it would be until the pharmacy got one in. I could do nothing more than trust that God would again provide my every need even when the odds seemed stacked against me in this situation.

That was a very rough night as I was (again) up all night coughing, gasping for breath and wheezing severely. The next day, God provided and the pharmacy obtained a donated inhaler for me. I was thanking the Lord and praying for God's blessings on that person who donated a much-needed medication that I could not obtain myself! Every month from here on out, I would have to pray for an inhaler to be available that month until the pharmaceutical company decided whether or not I qualified for their patient assistance program, in which case I could get a three-month supply affordably through the pharmaceutical company.

I had doubts that I would even qualify because I was told that some pharmaceutical companies have strict income level guidelines that I would not meet. However, I at least had to apply so that I could more easily acquire the inhaler that I needed each month instead of having to depend on donated samples.

A few weeks later, the week of Christmas, my son came down with mono and the flu at the same time. We ended up in the emergency room late one Sunday afternoon and he needed several medications for that. Besides most of us feeling bad, the extra medical bills took away from the "festivities of the season."

Even the dog wanted to get in on the "fun" by developing a palsy on one side of her face causing her eye to droop along with an eye infection, which meant more medications were needed along as well as an unexpected vet bill. However, at least my youngest son managed to stay healthy throughout the season, and that was something to be thankful for!

Because of all of these unexpected expenses (my spinal tap bill, the medications and office visit for my sinus infection and bronchitis, my son's medications for the flu and mono, and the vet bills), I had to dip into my

Christmas fund, which was meager at best. My heart sunk realizing how hard I had to save and a lot of it had to go towards these unexpected bills. However, I remembered how God had provided for Christmases past, and I knew He could again…and He did! He is so faithful! Even better, I was able to have every last medical bill paid off by March, a mathematical impossibility considering how little was coming in and how much had to go out!

While all of this was going on, my mom called and told me she had just been diagnosed with Parkinson's disease. I became concerned about her as she lives alone and so far away from most of the family. However, I was grateful at that moment that I had just had the opportunity to see her for Thanksgiving the month before. She had aged many years since the last time I had seen her, which had been about four years prior to this visit. She did not look the same or act the same; though she looked like my mom, she wasn't the same mom I remembered. It broke my heart to see her in this condition. (However, she has since started a medication for it and is doing remarkably better).

The week my mom called with this diagnosis was the same week as my birthday and also the same week that my Multiple Sclerosis diagnosis was confirmed. My neurologist reminded me at this time that MS can be a debilitating disease (which I knew) and also very expensive (not the best time to get all of this news at once). She then gave me the choice of whether or not to start the medication at this time (daily injections), which she said was very expensive and would make me feel quite sick for the first three months or so until my body adjusted to it and could cause some nasty side effects. Because I was still trying to battle my way through asthmatic bronchitis, a sinus infection, the news I had just received about my mom, and now this news, I told her I wanted to wait on the medication for now and just keep a close eye on the progression of the disease before committing to this regimen.

Although this was difficult news to get, God had been gracious enough to prepare me well long beforehand so that it was not a big shock when I got the confirmed diagnosis. Still, my heart sank because I was hoping the doctors would find some other, more easily manageable problem, and then I could go on with my life as before.

As I was going through all of this illness and financial stress, the Lord laid **II Chronicles 20:15-23** on my heart. Everywhere I turned, references to these verses were there; there was no escaping it! These verses directly related to what I was facing that particular month and really encouraged me and strengthened me throughout this battle and state in part, *"Do not be afraid or discouraged because of this vast army. For the battle is not yours, but God's. Go out to face them tomorrow, and the Lord will be with you...As they* began to sing and praise Him, *the Lord set ambushes against the men who were invading Judah and they were defeated."* (NIV) I posted all of these verses in full on my bathroom mirror where I could look at them every day to gain strength. They encouraged me to remember that I was not alone in the battle, but that God was fighting with and for me! My job was to praise Him, trust Him and keep moving forward, and He would take care of the rest!

When I finally began to feel better physically, I went out late one evening to the grocery store. One of my closest friends called me on my way to the store, and I said I would call her back within thirty minutes. When I came out of the store, I reached in my purse for my phone, and it was gone. I had just talked to my friend on my way there, so I thought maybe I had just left the phone in the car. I searched every inch of the car, including under the seats, but the phone was not there. I emptied my purse out, and it was not in there either. Then I thought maybe I had put it down in the store while looking at something. I retraced all my steps in the store, but it was nowhere to be found! Some of the employees helped me search and even called my number, but it never rang. I never saw my phone again after that. In any case, I not only lost a phone that I now had to replace (another unexpected expense), but I lost all of my pictures, contacts and most importantly, some texts I had received from a friend right before she passed away just a few months prior. Those precious messages were now gone forever.

For a few weeks after this happened, things seemed to calm down until I backed into the mailbox and did $1800 of damage to my car. Never before had I backed into anything with my car to cause any damage, but this time I really did it! It was unbelievable the amount of damage that little mailbox did! Although I was sick at how badly the car looked and that now

I would have car repair bills, at least the mailbox was still standing, and I did not have to replace that, too! I usually try to find the silver lining in bad situations, and there it was although small!

By this point, I was quite overwhelmed financially and physically and began to feel very alone. I did not have much support after getting my diagnosis of MS and if anything, a lot of people backed away and did not say anything about it. Maybe they did not know what to say or maybe a lot of people do not know what MS is or the potential seriousness of the disease, especially when I looked perfectly fine on the outside. However, on the inside I felt anything but fine.

It just takes a small act of kindness, such as a hug or hearing that someone is praying for you to help when facing something like this. Even a quick text saying that someone is thinking about you means a lot. It is often said that you find out who your true friends are when you are faced with a difficult valley in your life, and I found out how FEW true blue friends I really had. It really hit me hard considering I always had a plethora of friends all around me just prior to this news.

However, my immediate and extended family was very supportive, and I was very thankful for them, who, even though I rarely got to see them, reached out to me more than they ever had before. Also, the teachers at the boys' school often told me they were all praying for me whenever they met for prayer, and this was an invaluable source of encouragement and comfort to me. One of the teachers sensed I was having a rough time of it, though I tried hard not to come off that way, and simply said, "How are you REALLY doing? I think you just need a hug" and she proceeded to give me a hug. This was much needed at that moment, more than she realized. That one simple act reached to my very core as I realized at that one moment that even though many people did not seem to care what I was going through at my lowest, at least one person truly did and was bold enough to show it.

A new battle began to settle in soon after....depression. I had never once had an episode of depression since I was a teenager, so this was new territory. The loneliness was unbelievable and was the precipitating factor for the depression. That is one downfall of being a person who really loves and cares about others. Because I felt so alone in all of this, I became hurt and angry at people for walking away when I needed them the most. One lesson I had to learn was that I could not expect people to care and respond to me in the way I would to them had they found out bad news or were going through a really tough time. I had to pray earnestly through that hurt and anger because that was the last emotion I wanted or needed to feel at this time.

I know it sounds ironic, but I began to withdraw from people at this point. All I wanted to do was stay home, lock myself in my bedroom and cry my eyes out. Although I loved my job, it became a chore to drag myself to work every day, and I did not even want to step foot into my church. It took everything within me to muster up the courage to step in through the door. I knew that was Satan hard at work on me emotionally and mentally because I have never felt that way before; I loved going to church and I knew that it was the place I needed to be the most through this time.

Loneliness, financial stress and physical illness are a very difficult combination and just the perfect storm that Satan needed to discourage me emotionally and mentally to the point where I began to lose hope. Even the promise that God had given me the year previous to this (**Jeremiah 29:11**) seemed an impossibility. For a short moment when I hit the lowest point in all of this, I felt that God had NO plans for my life and that surely there was nothing great about my future if this was how it was going to be.

Some new feelings and thoughts that I was unprepared for hit me hard all at once, but I remembered back to what the Lord had reminded me of previously to this storm. My hope is in Him alone and that I needed to rest in Him and trust Him. Even though THIS was the heart of the battle and the most difficult part, the battle of the mind and emotions, I also knew without a doubt that God would see me through it because He told me He would.

Again, the Lord reminded me this was not my battle to fight alone. He had prepared me for it ahead of time, He would be there with me through it fighting alongside me and He would see me through to the end of it also. Everything He had prepared me for the previous year made perfect sense now. However, the seven-week depression was still an extremely difficult period and there were two times I was at the verge giving up. Had it not been for my kids and a special pastor on staff at my church who texted encouraging messages saying he was, "praying for me on the spot that God would step in and show Himself strong" (in my weakness) and telling me he was "standing with me in prayer believing that God would do great things (for me)," I think I would have given up the fight at this point.

I was completely worn; I had no more fight left to give. I even felt too weak to have words to pray, but God knew the words in my heart that I could not even speak out loud. (**"The Spirit helps us in our weakness. We do not know what we ought to pray for, but the Spirit himself intercedes for us with groans that words cannot express." Romans 8:25).** All I could do was picture myself resting in His arms of love and trust Him to carry me through the rest of this battle. The GREAT news is that God is the strength in our weakness (**II Corinthians 12:9**), and He does not expect us to go it alone; He understands when we are even too weak to say anything but "Jesus."

Throughout all of these difficulties, The Lord took me to a new level of faith. I fully believed that God was always there with me and never left me, but throughout this battle, there were times when I did not even feel God's presence as I normally do and that scared me. However, looking back, I believe that the Lord was testing my faith to see if I was going to believe that He was still there even when I did not feel Him there. I had to **choose to believe** in the darkest moments when I felt totally alone that He was, in fact, still there because His Word says He is always there, even if everything within me did not **feel** it. When I chose to believe He was there despite how I felt, my footing in the hardest places became a little stronger and then my doubts began to fade as to whether or not I would make it through this battle.

Nevertheless, I still had some work to do on PRAISING God through the storms. It is very important not to merely live in survival mode through these times, but to praise God through these times, because He is STILL worthy of all glory and praise regardless of what we face or how we feel. **Luke 19:40** says, "…if they (we) keep quiet, the stones will cry out." (NIV) His praiseworthiness is **not** based on our circumstances, good or bad, but because of who He is.

After this short period of depression, I began to have some good days. As I breathed a sigh of relief thinking this trial was over, the Lord whispered "It's not over yet." Though I became very discouraged again at that point,

I knew He would not leave me now, because He had brought me this far (I was still alive and intact) and I knew that He would see me through the rest of it, too.

During this "phase" of my battle, we lost our beloved dog which we had had for almost eleven years. She had been with us since the boys were little and was a source of great comfort through my divorce.

She was getting up in age at this point, and it appeared she was having a more difficult time getting around. I thought she was having more trouble with arthritis. When I took her to the vet on a Monday, I was told her red blood cell count was critically low. After several tests and blood work, I found out that her white blood cell count and marrow counts were very low also. We tried to give her steroids, antibiotics and anti-inflammatories to try to bring her count back up, but by then it was too late.

When her other blood work came back from the lab the next day, it looked like cancer. Four days after her vet visit, she was gone. She was barely able to lift her head up that week and went downhill very quickly. Because the boys were out of town, I knew she was trying to hang on to life until they got back, but she just couldn't. I reassured her that it was okay to go. She was in extreme pain, and it was too hard to watch her suffer so much. At first I prayed that she would make it until the boys came home in order for them to say goodbye; then I prayed that God would take her very quickly. I cried profusely off and on all week as I was hoping to have her around for another couple of years, but yet I did not want her to suffer so much either. She had two seizures on that Thursday and then died in my arms. God had graciously taken her quickly. This was painful beyond words, but it was for the best and I did not have to watch her suffer for very long.

I am convinced that heaven got a doggie angel that day. She was one of the best things that ever happened to us, and we were blessed beyond words by getting to have her for almost eleven years. I had never felt a pain so sharp within my heart before; it felt like I lost a family member. Although I had sensed in my spirit a few weeks prior to this that death was somehow going to touch our family, I was still not prepared for that kind of pain. What made it more difficult was that the boys were out of town, and I was home alone. The house was too quiet without her and them. Again,

God provided for me, and a dear friend from church came and stayed with me for a few days until the boys got home. Just having someone there with me to help those quiet, lonely hours pass by just hanging out and talking was a huge blessing and one I will never forget!

A few months before my dog's death, I had begun to lose interest in everything. I felt like I had lost the passion that had driven me over the past forty years. I could not explain it but figured it had to be another one of Satan's attacks as this was a 180 degree turn from who I normally am. One of the most dangerous places to be is to stop caring about anything and losing passion for everything that used to be enjoyable and not even know why or how. I knew that once again I had to fight and pray hard to regain that passion; I was determined not to give up that easily. It was a tug-of-war battle for months, but I knew that together the Lord and I would win this battle, too.

I significantly cut back on social activities and began to stay at home a lot more. Though sometimes I got bored, I still did not want to do anything that I normally enjoyed doing. I did not even care when my house was in shambles, which is very unlike me. I did not want to go anywhere, read or write anything, have anyone over for dinner, talk to my friends on the phone, or even bake anymore, which had been some of my favorite things to do. The things I used to get excited about did not even affect me. I did not even look forward to things that I normally would have been ecstatic about. The depression had subsided, but I simply felt like the excitement for life had been drained out of me.

Again, I reread all of the things I had written down from the previous year that the Lord used to prepare me for this battle. I once again claimed the Scriptures that kept pulling me "back on track" throughout this time and encouraged me to keep going. It seemed that the worst was over, yet I was also miserable. The last thing I wanted to lose was my God-given passion and drive for people, life and causes that mattered.

Even though I did my best to keep my chin up through this battle while I was at work, my boss noticed my lack of passion and enthusiasm for my job. I did not think that it had become this obvious to others, and it really surprised me that he had noticed since I did not even work closely with him during the day. I was thankful that he was very understanding, gracious and kind. He was aware that it had been a very difficult year for me and took that into consideration.

Through this four-month period of "lifelessness," I had to deliberately, consciously picture God's army around these "GIANTS" that surrounded me because it was so hard to see through the darkness of the valley. I was temporarily blinded to God's army and desperately prayed that God would give ME eyes to see His army because He already told me **this was His battle and not mine**. Throughout this period, God continued to encourage me with very specific promises out of Scripture to gradually help me fight through this and regain my passion for life again.

At just the perfect time, my boys had a special service at their school where a guest preacher came and spoke. The Lord really encouraged me to keep on going strong and not give up the race as the preacher spoke on **I Corinthians 9:24 and 25** which state, *"Do you not know that in a race all the runners run, but only one gets the prize? Run in such a way as to get the prize. Everyone who competes in the games goes into strict training. They do it to get a crown that will not last; but we do it to get a crown that will last forever."* (NIV) This message could not have come at a better time than this! I was still feeling weakened from the last several months of having been through the biggest battle in my life. However, I was comforted by the fact that God Himself was encouraging me through His Word at just the perfect time as He has done many times before. Though I still struggled off and on with this for a few more months after that, this was just the boost I needed to jump-start my passion for life once again.

That was the beginning of the end of this season of intense battle. I gradually began to have more good days when I felt stronger and more like myself again. I still thank God for His love and grace that got me through this dark valley. I literally would not have made it without His year of preparation and the strength He gave me at every turn to keep me going one more day!

On one of my good days coming out of this battle, I noticed something different as I drove through the same section of trees that I have driven through for the past five years every day to and from work. The sun was out, and it was a beautiful day. It suddenly hit me how tall and strong the trees were, unmoved and unchanged by everything around them. Even though we get a lot of bad storms here, they stood as if no storm had ever come through. Although my life had been turned upside down through my great storm, God's strength also helped me remain intact and unmoved, just like those trees.

What hit me at that point was that God, too, stays the same even when we face great difficulties in life. That gave me such comfort and peace, knowing that there was strength and stability all around me that did not change even when I felt like the rug was pulled out from underneath me. God is the same yesterday, today and forever. No matter what we lose, how much we suffer, how beaten down we feel, and how weak we become, He is the same gracious, loving, and kind God that He has always been. Even if we don't feel Him at our lowest moments, He promises us that He will always be there for us and with us.

I am thankful beyond words that the Lord has graciously brought me through the most difficult battle of my life! My faith, though strong before this battle, grew to a new level, and I now feel an even more deep-rooted peace, confidence and stability than before. Because of the strength God gave me in my weakness, I have come out on the other side stronger than before. I also feel better prepared for whatever happens in the future, knowing I can and will come out through it stronger and better, not destroyed or worse off. I know this because of the One who lives in me and the fact that He is stronger than any battle, illness, or loss that I face.

"Be still and know that I am God."
Psalm 46:10

Chapter 14

I am the LORD That Heals You

One of the things I learned this past year was that there is a BIG difference between believing that God CAN heal you and that God WILL heal you! Of course He CAN heal because He is all powerful; nothing is impossible for Him! However, it takes a bold step of faith to declare that God is GOING to heal you, and not that He merely has the power to do so, a much safer and easier thing to believe.

Besides the aforementioned healings in Chapter 12, there were three more specific healings that God performed in my body throughout the next two years. Once I saw and felt first-hand how God had worked miraculously in my body by completely restoring lost strength in my legs and then healing the severe stiffness and excruciating pain in my spine, it was very easy for me to believe that God would continue to heal my body until it was completely restored; after all, He never does anything half-way! I excitedly anticipated the rest of my healing, which would surely come.

During the summer of 2013, I again spoke to a group of guys in a residential recovery program that I regularly spoke to, sharing another one of my testimonies. This particular time, I shared how God had so meticulously prepared me for the intense battle I had faced, the major details of the battle and how God had so faithfully encouraged me and stayed with me through the battle. One of the major points I shared was that it does not matter how we feel during the battles, God is with us and for us, even if we do not sense his presence. When feelings deceive us, we need to accept God's promises in His Word by *faith* and stand on those promises to get us through the hardest battles.

After I shared my testimony with them, they asked to lay hands on me and pray over me for my physical healing, particularly the Multiple Sclerosis. I was so touched by their willingness and desire to pray for me; I was there to minister to them and certainly did not expect this kind gesture. However, they ministered to me even more that night! Within a few days, my tremors, which had increased over a period of the last three years until they were a daily problem, drastically reduced by about 85% or so and continued to slowly decrease over time after that. Though I still have occasional episodes of tremor in my hands or core, they are not daily or nearly as intense as they had been before that night.

I am not sure why, but God has chosen to heal me slowly over time in stages. I noticed that in every case, my physical issues that He healed in particular had gotten worse right before His healing took place.

About the same time as this healing of my tremors, I began to develop increasing problems with breathing. I just assumed my asthma had gotten worse as the summer weather began, so I went to my doctor to see if something else could be done to help. I was given a breathing test, and my doctor said it was normal but did give me a prescription for medication to take along with my inhaler to see if that would open my bronchial passages a little more. However, after being on it for two months, I did not notice a bit of difference, so I discontinued it.

The summer months are always more difficult on my asthma, especially the 100 degree days! I continued to have difficulties catching my breath in the middle of talking and sometimes even while walking across the house or out to the car after work. I decided to wait and see how my asthma reacted when the temperature started cooling down, thinking that would solve the problem. However, nothing changed with the cooler weather. Along with the breathing difficulties, I also began to have a sharp pain in the upper part of my middle back which felt stabbing, like a knife, at times. I felt these two problems may have been somehow related.

I felt I had already exhausted my possibilities with my last doctor's appointment and I was unsure what to do from that point, so I began to pray about where to go from here. Soon afterwards, I heard a still small voice that said, "You need to go see a chiropractor. Go see Jeff," an acquaintance who is a chiropractor. I had never even thought of going that route, as I was somewhat of a skeptic when it came to that kind of thing. However, I knew that the Lord was telling me I needed to go, so I went in faith knowing that it certainly could not hurt at this point; hopefully I would now find out the answer to my newly developed spinal pain and breathing problems.

The chiropractor took some x-rays of my spine while I was standing up. I had just had x-rays of my entire spine while lying down at the clinic, which had masked the problem in the thoracic area of my spine because nothing was found where most of my pain was at that particular time. However, the pain told me otherwise and I knew something was not right. The chiropractor discovered that I had kyphosis, a condition in which my thoracic spine was curving inwards, which over time slowly begins caving in on itself. This was putting pressure on my lungs, making it difficult for them to fully inflate. It was then that I told Jeff that I had been experiencing increasing breathing problems over the previous five or six months and now I finally had my answer as to why! This was also causing the sharp pain in that area as well.

The chiropractor also reiterated what I already knew from working for doctors who treated spinal problems, that I had the spine of somebody in their 60s though I was only in my early 40s! It was difficult to see the problems on the outside (although I could certainly feel it!) and he was very surprised that my entire spine was in as bad of shape as it was after seeing what it looked like on the inside.

I was very relieved to know what the problem was now and that it was not merely in my head. Because treatment would have to be intense for six months because of all of the problems in my spine, it was going to cost thousands of dollars to get it treated chiropractically. Obviously, this would be an impossibility in my financial situation; I would either need a financial miracle (after all, He owns the cattle on a thousand hills) or another healing miracle (and I have seen Him do these already!)

I was incredibly thankful that at least I now knew what to pray for specifically in my personal prayer time as well as the next time we had prayer at church for healing. Just a few weeks later the opportunity came, and I could not get to the front of the church fast enough for prayer for the kyphosis and accompanying breathing problem. I asked one of the pastors to pray specifically for those problems, because I was feeling absolutely miserable! That night was the worst pain and breathing difficulty up to that point, yet I did not let that discourage me because I believed my healing was literally right around the corner!

Sure enough, I woke up around 4:00 a.m. that very night, and I could take a deep breath for the first time in almost six months! I sat up in bed and kept breathing in as deeply as I could, utterly amazed at the difference from just the evening before! Also, the sharp stabbing pain in my upper middle back was much better and no longer constant.

Even though I could now take in a full breath, something I had been unable to do for about six months prior to this healing, I still had the wheezing and chronic cough associated with my asthma. They were two separate problems but now the most bothersome problem was healed. Now I could focus my attention on the asthma. I believed that because God healed the other breathing problem, He would heal my asthma too. About a month later, we had another special healing service at church, and I went up to be anointed and then prayed over for healing of my asthma, my MS and my remaining spinal problems. I was very excited as I went up there, knowing that God was going to heal one, if not all, of these physical conditions.

That night I opted to skip my inhaler, trusting that God was going to at least heal my asthma that night. Every other time when I had skipped a dose, my wheezing substantially increased as did the cough. However, when I woke up the very next morning, the wheezing was completely gone! I also noticed later that week that my chronic cough was also gone! Although this chronic cough had been kept under control for the most part, it had been a problem for over three years and never went completely away, even with asthma medication or the inhaler. I have not had to use my inhaler or asthma medication since, and to date it has been over three months since I last used them. Praise God!!

Sometimes, God heals us medically through health care professionals and other times He heals us instantly and miraculously by His powerful touch. My prayer is that you don't become discouraged if the doctors say there is nothing they can do for you or they do not spend the time required to get to the root of the problem, or if you do not have the financial means to get the problem fixed or treated. The Great Physician treats miraculously, does not treat anyone like a number, can heal instantly and completely and does not cost a dime! He will not turn you away because He is too busy with "other patients" or because you do not have the money to get treatment. When you combine your faith with God's compassion, love and grace, there is nothing He cannot or will not heal.

You may ask, "What about those who have faith they can be healed and they aren't healed," or "What about my friend who was not healed and died as a result?" I, too, have had friends die of cancer who had faith in God and that He could do the impossible. As a human seeing things from a human perspective, I cannot answer that question. Only God knows the answer to that. There are many unanswered questions we will not understand while we still live on earth, but even so, it is important to have faith that God is able to do, *"immeasurably more than all we ask or imagine, according to His power that is at work within us..."* **Ephesians 3:20** (NIV).

CHAPTER 15

Growth and Restoration
Psalm 71:20-21

Although my life has been inundated with trials, it has truly been an adventure! I would not be the strong person I am today nor would my faith be as strong, valuable or precious as it is to me had it not been for the storms I went through. I would not have had the amazing opportunities to see how strong and faithful my God is had everything in my life gone smoothly.

By being "struck down, but not destroyed" over and over, my faith has grown rock-solid. However, this came with much time and through much difficulty as I matured in my walk with the Lord. Earlier on in my walk, there were times when my faith was tested and shaken up. Time and time again, as the Lord brought me through those trials and encouraged me through them, my faith grew a bit stronger after each trial when I had seen the amazing ways God brought me through each one. There were times through that process when I even questioned whether or not God saw or cared what I was going through, only to see Him waiting on the other side. Through those experiences, I learned how to recognize when the enemy, who is the Father of all Lies, was working overtime to discourage me by blurring my eyes to the truth.

Psalm 71:20-21 states, *"Though you have made me see troubles, many and bitter, you will restore my life again; from the depths of the earth you will* *again bring me up. You will increase my honor and comfort me once again."* (NIV) Troubles are a guaranteed part of this life, because sin entered into the world. Nowhere does the Bible say that life will be easy and trouble-free; it only says that there will be those times when life is very difficult, but the Lord promises to walk with us through those times. Ironically, God often uses those troubles to create something beautiful out of our lives. In one way or another, He will restore us and make us stronger through the difficulties. We also learn how to rely on Him more through those times, and less on ourselves. Think about it. If life were easy, would we really have a desperate need for God in our lives? And, would we have a longing for heaven, our real home, if our lives here on earth were always splendid? Probably not.

If you do not have a relationship with God, would you like to know him better? This God, who is the ultimate restorer, protector, friend, strong tower and deliverer, loves you more than you can imagine! He longs for a relationship with you so much that he sent His only Son Jesus to this troubled, sin-filled earth to die for your sins! He took on Himself the burden and shame of all our sins so that we can be reconciled to God, for God is so Holy that He is unable to even look upon us because of our sin. There is only one way to heaven; through His Son Jesus Christ. **John 3:16-17** says this best, *"For God so loved the world that He gave His one and only Son, that whoever believes in Him shall not perish but have eternal life. For God did not send His Son into the world to condemn the world, but to save the world through Him."* (NIV)

Many people know who God is and may even have **head** knowledge of the Bible and fear Him because they know His power. However, even the demons have this knowledge and tremble! Truly knowing God is much more than just having common knowledge; it is all about having **heart** knowledge…and a relationship with Him. When somebody truly has a relationship with the Lord, there is a definite change in that person's life from who they were before. And just like any other good relationship, it takes time and commitment to make the relationship grow.

If you have not done so, I encourage you to seek a relationship with Jesus Christ. I know a lot of people personally, who, like myself would never have survived some very difficult times without this precious relationship.

He is the most faithful, loving friend you will ever have! When others let you down, and everybody will at one time or another, He will still be there. I can truly say from experience that even though my life has seen much more than its fair share of difficulties, having the Lord in my life has been the GREATEST adventure, unequaled by anything the world could possibly offer me!

How do you seek a relationship with Christ? First, ask Him to come into your heart and life and change you from the inside out. Admit your need for Him in your life; none of us can make it through this difficult life without Him. Next, sincerely acknowledge that you believe Jesus died for you and that His blood alone pays for your sins once and for all as you confess and forsake your sins. Salvation is His **gift** to you, not something you can earn on your own. We could never possibly do enough good things to get ourselves into heaven. Thirdly, receive that gift **by faith** and acknowledge Him as your Lord and Savior. Now get ready for the greatest adventure you could ever imagine!

I would love to hear how these testimonies have encouraged you or touched your life! Please email me at marie.Rosebook@yahoo.com.

Visit my blog at: www.marierosebook.blogspot.com

Study Guide

Chapter 1

1. How did your childhood affect your outlook on life as an adult? Did it give you a positive or negative outlook on life in general?
2. How did your relationship with your earthly father shape your view of God, your Heavenly Father? In what ways was your earthly father a reflection of God? If your father was uninvolved in your life as a child, did that negatively affect your view of God? Is that a fair and accurate view of who God really is?
3. Looking back on your childhood, can you see how God used your experiences (whether good or bad) to shape who you are today? How?
4. What particular experience in your childhood had the greatest impact on your life as an adult?
5. If you had a relationship with God as a child, what things did God help you overcome throughout your childhood and adolescent years? If you did not have a relationship with God as a child, how do you think things could have been different with God in your life?
6. His Word says that He is our refuge, strength, comforter, deliverer, restorer, hope and help! Give some examples of how He has been each one of these to you personally.

Chapter 2

1. Looking back, how do you think your friends influenced the way you lived and your attitudes in life? Did you have strong Christian friends to encourage and support you? Did you have any friends that you believe negatively influenced you and drew you away from God? What does that say about the importance of keeping good company?
2. Have you ever experienced living in another culture? If so, how has this influenced you? Has it made you a better person? Are you now more appreciative of what you have?
3. After praying about something specific, have you ever had to make a difficult decision that went against everything you wanted because you knew that it was what God wanted you to do? Did you ever find out later why God led you to make that decision? If not, do you still trust Him enough to know that He wants the best for you?
4. Sometimes we have to give up something good so that we can have God's best. Have you ever had to do this? In the end, did you see how God's best was well worth giving up what you thought was good?

Chapter 3

1. We all have important decisions to make. Have you ever made an important decision on your own without first consulting God? How did the outcome differ from another important decision you made after seeking God and waiting on His answer to guide you?
2. Many times God uses what others meant for evil in our lives for good in the end. Do you have a personal example where someone meant to harm you and it ended up turning around as a blessing? What examples can you think of in the Bible where this happened?
3. Has God set you free from bondage of any given thing in a unique way? Give an example. How did this magnify HIS name?
4. God is our mighty protector. When has He kept you safe in a potentially dangerous situation?

5. If you have had children, how has becoming a parent changed your relationship with your parents?
6. Sometimes, it is easy to look around at others and wonder why they don't struggle as much as we do. However, God uses these struggles in your life to shape you into the beautiful, special person you have become. What have you learned through a particular struggle in your life and how did it change you for the better?
7. Have you ever been betrayed by a spouse or friend? How did it feel? Remember, Jesus is the best friend you could ever have, and He will never leave, forsake or betray you! How can you take comfort in this fact?

Chapter 4

1. Are you or somebody you know married to someone with an addiction problem? If so, pray for that addict and their spouse! Encourage them every chance you get! Only God has the power to break the addiction and set them free, and only God has enough strength to carry their spouse through the difficulties that come from living with an addict, but you can be a very important part in bringing hope to those lives.
2. When have you put on a "good, happy face" at church but really felt sad or devastated on the inside? Is this how God wants us to be? Remember that our brothers and sisters in Christ are there to encourage us, build us up and pray for us so that we do not have to face these struggles alone!
3. How has God spoken to you or revealed Himself to you in such a powerful way that it changed you? If He has not done so, what can you do to draw closer to Him so that you too can experience this?
4. Give an example of when you completely gave something up to God and He lifted your heavy burden.
5. Have you ever had faith and believed that something was going to turn out a certain way but it ended up turning out differently? If so, how did that affect your faith? Even though something may not turn out "right" in your eyes, God sees the bigger picture and always has a plan B when YOUR plan A doesn't happen.

Chapter 5

1. Have you ever had to forgive somebody for really hurting you badly? Why is it so important to forgive that person, even if you don't want to?
2. Matthew 6:14 says that God will not forgive us our sins if we do not forgive others. Is there anybody in your life that you have not yet forgiven?
3. What are the benefits we receive when forgiving others?
4. Give an example of when God told you to wait on something. If you were obedient, what was the final outcome? If you were disobedient and acted quickly by making a rash decision, what was the final outcome?
5. What does the LORD promise to those that wait upon Him? (Isaiah 40:31)

Chapter 6

1. How has God orchestrated things to fall into place for you in a particular situation? How did that experience impact your faith?
2. It is absolutely essential that we pray and seek God's guidance before making important decisions. Give an example of a time when you: a) prayed beforehand and b) did not pray beforehand. What was the outcome each time? What did you learn as a result?
3. When has God the provider filled in the cracks financially where your income could not? How did His provision in that situation affect your faith?
4. Respond to this statement. When we faithfully tithe, He will provide our every need. Can you think of a time where it was difficult to tithe but you did so, and God blessed your obedience?
5. In what radical way has God provided for your needs above and beyond what you were expecting?

Chapter 7

1. Give a specific example of how God has spoken to you through a particular Scripture.
2. Have you ever lost something very dear to you, and God stepped in and showed you that He is all you really need? How did He show you this?
3. If you have ever faced a period of unemployment, what did you learn from that experience? In what ways did the Lord provide for you during that time?
4. How have "better, stronger plants" grown out of your trials?

Chapter 8

1. Have you ever unfairly judged somebody? How do you think it made them feel? Did that attitude bring honor to God?
2. Have you ever been on the receiving end of judgment by another person? How did that make you feel?
3. What is Jesus' attitude towards unbelieving sinners? What is His attitude towards the Christian when he/she commits a sin? How can we follow His example?
4. Too many people are fickle when it comes to loving others. They pick and choose who they are going to love and show kindness to, but then act indifferently towards everybody else. Is this God's way?
5. How can you specifically reach out and help somebody who has been divorced or is a single parent?
6. If you have been through a divorce, how has God made you stronger through it?

Chapter 9

1. Have you ever prayed for something with such great detail that when God answered this prayer very specifically, it greatly increased your faith?
2. God blesses us **so that** we can bless others. He also gives us comfort **so that** we can give comfort to others. Have you kept these

blessings to yourself, or passed them on to others in their time of need? If you have blessed or comforted others as a result, how?
3. What good gifts has God blessed you with? Have you acknowledged that EVERY good gift comes from above? If not, start today and see how things change.
4. How has God opened doors for you so that what seemed impossible became possible?
5. Today, have you remembered to thank YAHWEH YIREH, your provider, for everything?

Chapter 10

1. Have you ever inadvertently tied part of your value to anything else besides God? Did you learn an important lesson from that?
2. Our society places value on us based on our looks, successes and money. Unfortunately, some people do not "measure up" and may feel that they have no value. How can we as Christians encourage them to see what their value is really based on?
3. In what specific way has God showed you hope during a "hopeless" situation? How did that affect your outlook on the situation?
4. In what ways have you grown in your walk with Christ as a result of going through a difficult waiting period?

Chapter 11

1. Have you or a loved one ever been anointed with oil? What miracles have you seen as a result?
2. When the future seemed bleak in the middle of a crisis, how did God step in to bring immediate comfort and reassurance?
3. Just as I cried out to Jesus during a crisis and the following week saw my name in flashing letters along with the words, "Jesus Loves You," on a church sign, in what mysterious way has the Lord made His presence known to you during or immediately after a crisis?
4. How has YAHWEH ROPHE specifically healed you? How did that healing affect your faith and the faith of others around you?

Chapter 12

1. Describe a time when you had a "breakthrough moment."
2. Is there something that you used to take for granted but now really appreciate it? If not, is there anything you can think of that you would like to begin thanking God for on a regular basis, such as your health, your house, your job, etc.?
3. God wants for us to trust Him fully in every situation. Is there a particular area in your life where you could trust Him more?
4. The Bible says "Do not fear" or "Fear not" 365 times, one for each day! What is it that you personally fear? Determine to make a commitment to not fear but instead trust God to help you overcome this fear.
5. It takes much more faith to believe God WILL do something and claim it done even before you have seen it, than to believe He CAN do something. What is one thing that you will claim already done, believing that God WILL do for you and thank Him ahead of time for it?
6. Give an example of something you had no peace about until you prayed and God gave you peace about it. What was the outcome?
7. Give an example of a battle you faced, but overcame with God's help.

Chapter 13

1. Find some verses that you could use to encourage you when you face difficult situations down the road. Write them down and work on memorizing these.
2. Recall a time when God came through for you when all the odds were stacked against you and you did not see a way out.
3. At one point, I realized my job during this difficult battle was to praise Him, trust Him and keep moving forward and believe that He would come through for me. What circumstance in your life are you facing where you could adopt this attitude, believing that He will come through for you too?

4. The Bible tells us not to be afraid or discouraged, because He is with us and fighting for us. In what area can you work at being less afraid and more trusting?
5. Who has made a big difference in your life when you were going through a hard time? Have you thanked them? If not, what could you do to thank them in a special way?
6. Sometimes, difficult situations can blind us to the truth. In what situation do you need to ask God to give you the eyes to see His army around your giants instead of only seeing the giants surrounding you?
7. The Lord encourages us through difficult times so we can encourage others through their difficult times. Who is it that you can encourage this week?

Chapter 14

1. Is there a specific challenge you are facing right now where your focus needs to change from "I believe God can" to "I believe God will"?
2. Do you have a specific example of something God healed in your life (whether physically, emotionally or spiritually)?
3. In what ways is God's healing different from a physician's healing?
4. Choose a healing verse in the Bible and claim it daily as your own, believing that God WILL heal you.
5. Skim through the Gospels (Matthew, Mark, Luke and John), recording each healing that Jesus did and the circumstances around that healing as well as how He healed specifically in that situation and why. What does this teach you?

Chapter 15

1. When your faith has been tested, how have you responded?
2. When you are really discouraged in your faith, do you recognize that the enemy is behind it? If so, how do you counteract this discouragement? Do you pray through it until you are at peace?

3. How desperate are you for God? Is there something in your life that hinders you from being more desperate for Him? If so, what needs to change?
4. What is wrong with having head knowledge of God and His Word, but no heart knowledge?
5. What is the hardest thing that the Lord has asked you to do? Were you obedient? If so, what was the outcome?
6. What was the biggest lesson you learned by reading this collection of testimonies? Is there something you are going to do differently in your own life after reading this?

I would love to hear how these testimonies have encouraged you or touched your life! Please email me at <u>marie.Rosebook@yahoo.com</u>.

Visit my blog at: www.marierosebook.blogspot.com

Scripture References

Chapter 1
Psalm 27:10…Rededication
- II Corinthians 4:8
- Psalm 27:10
- Psalm 119:92
- Isaiah 9:6

Chapter 3
Our Honeymoon Years, in the Frigid North
- Psalm 127:3

Chapter 4
Sanctify Me
- Matthew 11:28
- Hebrews 11:1

Chapter 5
Lessons in Forgiveness
- Matthew 6:14-15
- Isaiah 41:9-10
- Isaiah 40:31 (KJV)

Chapter 6
Georgia-Bound!
- Revelation 3:7
- Matthew 11:28-30
- Matthew 6:25-26
- Psalm 147:4
- Psalm 17:14b
- Philippians 4:12-13

Chapter 7
Starting Over, With a Promise in Job 8
- Job 8:5-7, 18-22
- Matthew 5:4
- Psalm 37:25-26
- Habakkuk 3:17-18

Chapter 8
Thrown Stones
- John 8:7
- John 13:35
- Isaiah 41:10
- Isaiah 30:11
- Isaiah 40:29
- Romans 15:2-3, 7

Chapter 9
A New Home
- Matthew 7:11

Chapter 10
A "Hopeless" Situation Filled with Hope
- Job 11:18
- II Corinthians 1:3-4
- Matthew 6:28-30, 33-34
- Matthew 10:29-31

Chapter 11
YAHWEH ROPHE – The LORD Who Heals
- James 5:14-15

Chapter 12
A Year of Rest, Blessing & Preparation
- II Timothy 1:7 (KJV)
- Luke 8:48
- II Chronicles 20:15b, 17b
- Jeremiah 29:11

Chapter 13
The Battle Begins
- I John 4:4
- II Chronicles 20:15-23
- Jeremiah 29:11
- Romans 8:26
- II Corinthians 12:9
- Luke 19:40
- I Corinthians 9:24, 25
- Psalm 46:10

Chapter 14
I am the LORD That Heals You
- Ephesians 3:20

Chapter 15
Growth & Restoration
- Psalm 71:20-21
- John 3:16-17

Endnotes

1. Shust, Aaron, "My Hope is in You," *This is What We Believe,* **CD.** Centricity Music, 2010

2. David Crowder Band, "Never Let Go," *Remedy,* **CD.** sixstepsrecords, 2007

3. Calling Glory, "Don't Give Up," *Teach Me To Love,* **CD.** Soncured Records, November 9, 2011